Planets

☉	Sun
☽	Moon
☿	Mercury
♀	Venus
♂	Mars
♃	Jupiter
♄	Saturn
⚷	Chiron
♅	Uranus
♆	Neptune
♇	Pluto

Signs

♈	Aries
♉	Taurus
♊	Gemini
♋	Cancer
♌	Leo
♍	Virgo
♎	Libra
♏	Scorpio
♐	Sagittarius
♑	Capricorn
♒	Aquarius
♓	Pisces

Elements

🜂	Fire
🜃	Earth
🜁	Air
🜄	Water

Modes

⊞	Cardinal
⋈	Fixed
⊜	Mutable

Star Power

**A simple guide
to astrology for the
modern mystic**

Vanessa Montgomery

Hardie Grant

QUADRILLE

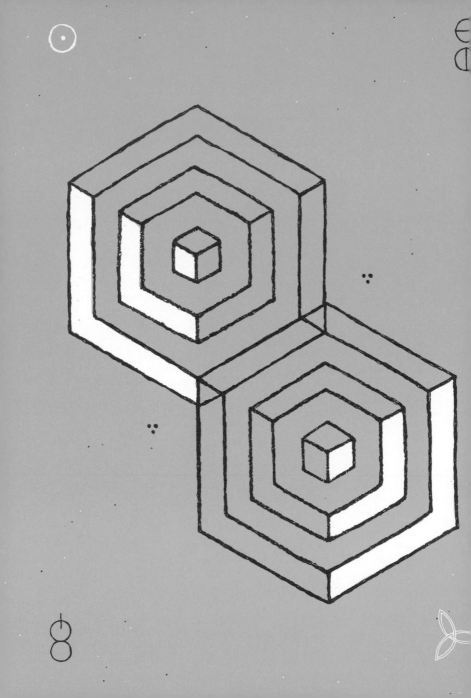

A brief history of astrology

We're ushering in an entirely new and exciting era of astrology. So many women are finding their inner modern mystic and tuning into a global spiritual awakening. We are becoming more empowered and finding ourselves in a privileged position: not only can we design and create our world, we can also redefine ourselves, our perceptions and our beliefs. There's a burgeoning awareness that we need to create inner balance so we can express our potential as individuals, and do it in a way that works in harmony with everyone else. This isn't a luxury, this is essential if we're to survive and thrive in a rapidly changing world. And astrology can provide us with the tools to do it.

Astrology essentially involves studying celestial objects – planets, moons, stars – and interpreting meaning from their movements and how they might affect everything in our Universe (including us!). It has been developed over thousands of years and its body of knowledge has been added to by many cultures; in the 21st century we have full access to this insightful system, which has been reloaded for the now-age woman.

The oldest known forms of celestial study and record-keeping are 32,000-year-old bone carvings and cave paintings of the Moon's phases. You may be surprised to learn that astrology drove the development of both astronomy and mathematics: for millennia, science and the arts were seen as one multifaceted system. But as the holistic view of life became separated into branches of study, this connection was lost.

A basic timeline follows the development of astrology from Mesopotamia in around 6000 BCE through ancient Egypt to Babylon in around 2400–331 BCE, then to Greece, on to the Roman Empire, Persia between 226 and 651 CE, Arabia from 750–950 CE, and finally to Britain and Europe in the Middle Ages, where the house division system that we use today was created. Its widespread recognition declined with the rise of the power of the Christian church but in India, Vedic astrology continued on an unbroken path and remains in use to this day.

Renewed interest in Western astrology came in the 19th

century along with a wave of non-denominational spiritualism, somewhat like the one we're experiencing now. 'Star sign' horoscopes appeared in tabloid newspapers in the 1930s and were the limit of what most people understood astrology to be – until recently. Early-to-mid-20th-century psychologists like Carl Jung merged astrology and psychology, developing psychological, humanistic astrology. This is the modern style we use today. In the 1960s and 70s, social consciousness shifted radically as a whole generation rejected restrictive cultural codes, with many revisiting and further developing astrology as a tool for self-exploration. The years 2011–2026 have the astrological mark of being an ultra-spiritual cycle, involving a mass awakening of women searching for deeper meaning in life. As we seek to understand our reality, we're embracing and further redefining astrology.

Over the centuries, organised religion has been threatened by the insights astrology offers, even going as far as banning its practise upon pain of death (it's that powerful!). Modern science and rationalism tried to push it further to the sidelines, but science itself is beginning to validate the intuitively metaphysical side of reality through advances in the field of quantum physics. We understand that everything at the core is moving energy, and is composed mostly of empty space. Finally, science is catching up with what the ancient mystics have known for millennia. The analogy with life is that everything is energy, emanating from a void which is the creative space. Hello age of Aquarius – enter the modern mystic!

Practical, psychological and cosmic, astrology is the ultimate selfie. It's a map to your inner psyche that spells out your strengths, weaknesses, potential, blind spots, complexes, and limiting perceptions. Knowledge is power! Which makes astrology a tool for self-reflection, a guide to how to best meet your potential in the world, relationships, career, finance, home and self-realisation. Discover your needs and you can attend to them, and communicate them more clearly to others.

Astrology helps us understand others and get along with them, and appreciate differences that once confounded us. Harness astro power for the inside scoop on anyone. Empower yourself with ancient knowledge for the modern woman!

Language of astrology

Don't worry about understanding all these definitions straightaway. Come back to them as you make your way through the book and use them as a reminder of what the terminology is referring to. Not all of these terms are used in the book, but you might come across them later in your astrological journey of discovery, so keep in touch with these pages. Soon, you'll be fluent in astro-speak!

Angular house · These are the first houses that appear on each quarter of a birth chart: they are the 1st, 4th, 7th and 10th Houses. Planets in these houses are bestowed more importance than the other houses, especially if they're at the very beginning of the house. They function with more power, immediacy and strength compared to planets found in the succedent and cadent houses.

Ascendant or Rising sign · This is the sign rising on the horizon line where the sky meets the Earth. It will be at a specific degree of that sign. The 1st House marks this point on a birth chart – so the sign on the cusp of the 1st House is your rising sign. The 1st House is always clearly marked, so you will quickly be able to identify your rising sign, and the degree rising will be marked alongside it. The rising sign represents the 'self' while the opposite house, the 7th, represents the 'other', or you in relationship to the other (see *descendant*). The rising sign is the face we initially present in new situations and what others see when they first meet us. It's like a mask or the window dressing of a shop, which doesn't necessarily represent all that's inside. Together with understanding the Sun and the Moon in your birth chart, the rising sign is a key component.

Aspect · A geometric angle between two points in a chart. Depending on the angle, the relationship between the two points will be different. The five major aspects are: conjunction, sextile, square, trine and opposition.

Astrology · The system and study of meaning behind the movement of particular heavenly bodies and points in the sky, and the influence they have on human affairs as well as the natural world and events. There are many branches of astrology with different focuses, such as modern/psychological astrology (the subject of this book), traditional astrology, horary astrology.

Birth chart / Natal chart / Horoscope · A snapshot of the Sun, Moon and planets (the sky) at the exact place and time of birth – each person has a unique birth chart depending on where and when they were born. It's depicted as a 2D circle with 12 pieces representing the zodiac signs. The chart begins on the left-hand horizon line that intersects the circle horizontally, known as the ascendant. The chart is read anti-clockwise from that point. Astrologers rarely use the term horoscope for a birth chart, instead shortening it to 'chart', 'birth chart' or 'natal chart'. 'Horo' means hour while 'scope' means view, so, simply, 'view of the hour'. The horoscope column you see in magazines is an interpretation of a chart calculated for that day, week or month. The birth chart is a horoscope specifically calculated for the time and place of birth of an individual.

Cadent house · These are the third and final houses of each quarter of a birth chart: they are 3rd, 6th, 9th and 12th Houses. The impact of planets in these houses is slightly reduced compared to the stronger angular and succedent houses. See also *angular house* and *succedent house*.

Cardinal · See *mode*

Conjunction · See *aspect*

Conscious effort *(a psychological term)* · Conscious effort is about purposefully and determinedly being aware of how you are expressing a planet's function, based on its placement by sign and aspect. This is particularly important if the function of the planet conflicts with the sign, or there is a difficult aspect with that planet. For example, Sun in Aquarius. The Sun's function is shining as an individual, while Aquarius rules groups. If you have your Sun in Aquarius, you'll need to apply conscious effort to balance your own needs (Sun) with those of the group (Aquarius).

Degree · Each sign covers 30° of the chart. Planets are located at a certain degree of a sign. House cusps are also located this way. Look for the small number between 0° and 29° next to each planet and house cusp, which tells you the degree it is from the nearest sign.

Descendant · This is the sign and degree setting on the horizon line where the sky meets the Earth. The cusp of the 7th House marks this point on a birth chart. See also *ascendant.*

Detriment · A planet in the sign opposite to the sign it rules, for example, Mars in Libra. In this instance, you need to apply conscious effort to make the most of the planet's function.

Dignity · A planet in the sign it rules, for example, Mars in Aries. In this instance, the planet functions at its best.

Disown or Project *(a psychological term)* · Sometimes we project our own unconscious emotions or perceptions onto another person, or disown them by refusing to take responsibility for them. For example, you perceive someone else as being angry, but in reality it's you that's angry, you're just not in touch with that emotion, as perhaps you don't accept that it's OK to feel angry. The ideal is to own and therefore integrate these traits.

Ecliptic · A band of sky that circles the Earth along the apparent path of the Sun. This band is divided into 12 x 30° sections, each of which is loosely based on the 12 major constellations the Sun travels through each year from Aries to Pisces.

Element · The elements are Fire, Earth, Air and Water. The elements describe basic psychological types of human behaviour, particularly perception and operation. There are three signs for each element.

Exalted / Exaltation · A planet in a particular sign in which it functions particularly well, similar to Dignity. A planet in the opposite sign of its exaltation is called 'fall'.

Express / Expression *(a psychological term)* · Expressing a planet or sign is to attend to the needs suggested by that planet or sign in your chart. In other words, to actively engage it and its function or purpose. Expressing can be unconscious or conscious. With conscious expression we are aware of and can work with our needs rather than being lost in them. When we know what our needs are it's easier to arrange our lives so they are met.

Fixed · See *mode*

Glyph · A pictographic used to represent a planet or sign. When reading the birth chart, these standard glyphs will be used. The classic image associated with a sign (such as scales for Libra), is a popular symbol rather than a glyph.

Horoscope · See *birth chart*

House · A birth chart is divided into 12 divisions called houses. Each represents specific areas of life and psychological function such as health, marriage and career. They are fixed in a fixed order – the 1st House always begins on the horizon line where the sky meets the Earth. But the size of each house will vary, unlike the signs, which are always equal sizes of 30° each.

House cusp · The house cusp is the beginning point of a house which will be at a particular degree of a sign. For example, you might see the 2nd House begins at 5° Aries – this is the cusp.

Integrate *(a psychological term)* · Bringing together conflicting parts of self, emotions or life so they become whole.

Luminary · The Sun and Moon are technically luminaries rather than planets, but the tendency is to refer to them as planets.

Mode or Modality · Also known as a 'quality'. The modes are Cardinal, Fixed and Mutable. These describe the basic endurance style, energetic and psychological approach of a sign. Each has a different style and expression: Cardinal (initiating energy), Fixed (staying power) and Mutable (changeable, adaptable).

Mutable · See *mode*

Opposition · See *aspect*

Orb (of influence) · The allotted degree of allowance for each aspect between planets or points in the chart to be considered in relationship with one another. Some aspects allow an orb of 10°, while others will be within 1° or 2° of exactness.

Planet · The planets are used in astrology to represent various archetypal aspects and functions of our psyche: for example, Venus represents love and relating to others. They indicate what is happening in the chart, like characters with distinct personalities.

Polarity · Each sign and house has an opposite on the circular birth chart, positioned directly across from it. Being in polarity means being at an extreme end of an archetype. When expressing in extreme the traits of one sign, for example, it's helpful to know the traits of the opposite sign. Expressing traits of the opposite sign brings a polarity into balance. For example, too much Leo can mean too much self-centredness. To bring it into balance, express traits from its opposite sign, Aquarius, which will mean detachment and taking the needs of the group into account.

Retrograde motion · When a planet appears to be moving backwards in the zodiac (as opposed to direct motion), due to relative orbiting speeds of Earth versus the other planets. It is effectively backtracking over a certain amount of degrees of a sign that it already covered in direct motion. The area it covered initially before backtracking is the 'retroshade' or 'shadow'.

Return · When a planet has orbited a full cycle of the zodiac and has returned to the exact point it began. A planet 'return' in a birth chart is when a planet is in the exact same position in the chart as it was when you were born.

Rising sign · See *ascendant*

Rising planets · These are planets in the 1st House rising on or near the horizon line, which is marked in a birth chart by the ascendant line and degree on which the 1st House begins.

Rulership / Rules / Ruling sign · Each zodiac sign is ruled by a planet. Some planets rule two signs, others only one. A planet is in rulership when it is in a sign that it rules. In this case, it has more strength and importance in the chart and allows the more positive qualities of the planet to express.

Sextile · See *aspect*

Sign or Sun sign or Zodiac · Any one of the 12-piece zodiac, from Aries through to Pisces, based loosely on existing constellations that circle the Earth along the ecliptic. When a planet is travelling through a particular sign, the planet's function is flavoured by that sign. We use signs to draw out more detail on the function of a planet that is within it.

Square · See *aspect*.

Succedent house · These are the middle houses of each quarter of a birth chart: they are the 2nd, 5th, 8th and 11th House. Planets found in these houses are of medium strength compared to the stronger position of the angular houses, and the weaker position of the cadent houses.

Transit · The movement of a planet through a sign, house or point in the chart, which reflects its movement in the sky. For example, Mars transiting Aries, or Mars transiting the 4th House.

Trine · See *aspect*

Unlocking your birth chart

Star Power is a step-by-step guide to learning to read a birth chart (also known as a natal chart or horoscope). Each chapter is like a building block on your journey of discovery, so it's best to read the book from front to back. Each chapter will reveal the components that make up astrology and show you how to read them together so you can use astrology as a system.

What is a birth chart?

A birth chart is based on the time, date and place of birth. Use the calculator at www.astroallstarz.com/birthchart to generate one. Or use any free, easy-to-use generators online.

This chart gives you the position of the planets and signs, your rising sign, the house positions, and the position of signs on house cusps and aspects, all as they were at the time of your birth. You can generate a chart for anyone as long as you know their birthday info. When you first see a chart, it will look confusing – a mass of lines and icons (these are actually called glyphs). But as you become more familiar with the glyphs it will come into focus.

Knowing how to read your birth chart will empower your inner mystic! Going well beyond a star sign (which is simply the zodiac sign the Sun was in when you were born), reading a chart will give you insight into yourself and others. It helps you to identify and highlight your strengths and weaknesses, temperament, personality and areas of opportunity. You can read anyone's birth chart to find out these things about them.

How to use this book

Start with the Planets chapter, understand the functions they represent. Then move on to the Signs chapter: learn about their personalities and characteristics. And then tackle the Houses chapter: familiarise yourself with the areas of life where you'll feel the impact (or the 'expression') of the planets and signs.

To dig deeper, read about modes, nodes, aspects and transits. This will give you an even greater understanding of your birth chart. Go as deep as you like. But stick with it! It will all start to slot together, and before you know it, you'll be reading a chart like a pro.

Keywords (and how to use them)

In this book, each planet, sign and house (as well as other features within the birth chart) have been assigned keywords. Get to know these keywords, as they are literally the key to unlocking astrology. The keywords are listed in bold type at the top of each relevant page.

As you go through the book, you'll find the keywords are sometimes used as a shorthand (within brackets) to help you understand the connections between the planets, signs and houses. For example, you might see something like Moon (emotions), or it might be the other way around, such as love (Venus) – soon, you'll know the keywords without having to reference them.

While each planet and sign in this book is written as a pure archetype (by keywords), remember we are all a synthesis of our parts. No one is just purely one sign, no one exists in a single area of life. Appreciate this, and you'll soon master the art of reading a birth chart.

Keep it simple, be instinctive

To keep it simple, always go back to keywords. And use astrology to guide your imagination and instinct. Let your intuition be your most valuable asset. Your gut always knows – as they say, 'First thought, best thought.' Catch it before your logical mind cuts in and tries to override any insights delivered by your mystical, all-knowing voice! A good rule of thumb is, if you feel an upward expansive shift in your body, go with it. If it's downward and contracting, apply the brakes. No matter what anyone else says, your truth is your own. Your inner mystic reserves the final say. Free your mind, own your power, change your world!

Example birth chart of...

Claire Howell, born
September 16, 1997
at 9:55pm in
Sydney, Australia

♈	Aries	☉	Sun
♉	Taurus	☽	Moon
♊	Gemini	☿	Mercury
♋	Cancer	♀	Venus
♌	Leo	♂	Mars
♍	Virgo	♃	Jupiter
♎	Libra	♄	Saturn
♏	Scorpio	⚷	Chiron
♐	Sagittarius	♅	Uranus
♑	Capricorn	♆	Neptune
♒	Aquarius	♇	Pluto
♓	Pisces		

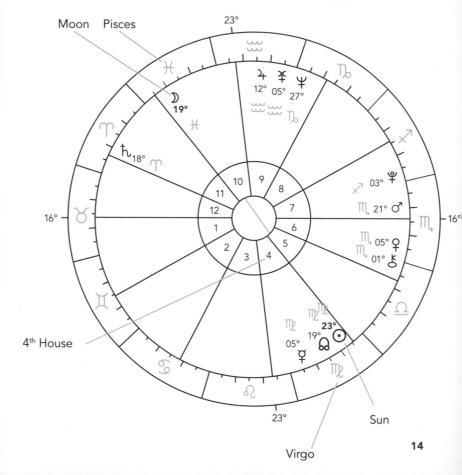

Navigating a birth chart

Reading a birth chart is a simple four-piece formula. The examples on these pages (based on one person's example birth chart) will make much more sense once you've read the book. You can familiarise yourself with the general principles, and/or come back to this chapter once you've made your way through the other chapters. Once you understand more about how to put the formula together, you can apply it to your own unique birth chart...

Planet
Identify the planet (eg Sun, Moon, Mercury, Jupiter etc)
These are positioned in the middle ring
And then note the keywords for that planet, see pages 24–67

+ Sign
Identify the sign the planet is in (eg within Aries, Cancer, Leo etc)
These are shown in the outer ring (and alongside the planet)
And then note the keywords for that sign, see pages 72–123

+ House
Identify the house the planet is in (eg within 2nd House, 5th, 7th etc)
These are indicated by the numbers in the central ring
And then note the keywords for that house, see page 140–163

+ Aspect
Identify if it forms an aspect (such as trine, square etc)
These are indicated by the degree (the little numbers)
alongside each planet and sign
*For more on understanding the degrees and aspects,
see pages 8 and 164–173*

Go through each planet using the formula above, starting with the Sun. Then work your way out to the outer planets. Add the elements and modes to reveal more!

A simple example based on Claire's chart on page 14

Planet Which planet?
Let's start with the Sun. The planets represent 'what' is happening in the chart – they are like the various characters representing parts of our psyche, each with a unique function.

+

Sign Which sign is the planet in?
The Sun is in Virgo. The sign a planet is in describes 'how' the planet expresses its unique function. In this case, the Sun is filtered through the qualities of Virgo.

+

House Which house is the planet in?
The Virgo Sun is in the 4th House. The house a planet is in indicates the particular area of life 'where' the planet is expressed. This is like the stage for the action taking place.

+

Aspects Is the planet forming any aspects?
The aspect looks at the relationship between the planets. In this case the Sun is forming an aspect to the Moon: they are 180° apart, and this aspect is called an 'opposition'. This means the Sun has opposite needs to Moon, which is in Pisces in the 10th House. So a balance must be struck between the needs of the Moon in Pisces and the needs of the Sun in Virgo.

=

In summary, the Sun is in Virgo in the 4th House, which is in opposition to the Moon in Pisces in the 10th House. Meaning that Claire's identity/self (Sun) needs order and detail (Virgo), especially in the setting of the home (4th House), which is in opposition to her emotional sustenance (Moon) derived from connecting through public image and career (10th House).

Further ways to unlock a birth chart

Rising sign / ascendant

The sign on the cusp of the 1st House is your rising sign. Take the rising sign as a focus (along with the Sun and Moon) when reading a birth chart. The rising sign is the face we initially present in new situations and what others see when they first meet us. It's like a mask or the window dressing of a shop, which doesn't necessarily represent all that's inside. The rising sign is like an overlay to our personality – so it can actually influence the way we look and present ourselves.

If your rising sign is very different to your Sun, Moon or Venus signs, people will often only see the real you once they've had time to get to know you. When we feel a bit ratty we tend to switch back to behaviour indicated by our rising sign as a defence mechanism.

Claire's rising sign is Taurus, which incidentally is ruled by Venus, so the position of Venus takes on even more importance in understanding Claire. Her Taurus rising will mean she has an appreciation of practical arts and beauty, as well as shopping and make-up or dressing up. Taurus rules the throat, so Taurus rising often indicates a pleasant voice and musical ability.

Balance of elements – high Earth, low Fire

What is the overall balance of elements in the chart? The personal planets (Sun to Mars) are the most revealing, together with the element of the rising sign.

Claire has the majority of her planets in Earth signs, plus her rising sign is Earth. This makes her a practical person seeking tangible results. She only has two planets in Fire signs, so she'll find herself compensating by importing Fire – as a professional performer, she thrives on attention from her audience, which brings in that life force of Fire.

Modes – high Mutable, high Fixed, low Cardinal

Now check the modes: is there an overwhelming influence of one mode? Claire has a lot planets in both Mutable and Fixed signs with only one in a Cardinal sign. She is very versatile (Mutable) and able to maintain effort over the long haul (Fixed).

Area of focus
Is there a cluster of planets (called a stellium) ganging up in one house of the chart, or across one quarter or half of the chart? Or are they spread out evenly? If one area is dominated, then read it as a focal point of your life. Claire's chart doesn't have a stellium.

Practise
Expand your experience by looking up as many people's charts as you can, including celebrities or a favourite mentor. This way you'll notice the similarities and differences, gain confidence and build your knowledge.

A more in-depth example based on Claire's chart

This is one to return to once you've read the book and understand the significance of each part of the birth chart, as well as follow the formula.

Planet Let's focus on Venus (beauty, relationships, love, values). Claire's Venus will tell us about her love style and needs, how she relates to other people and what her values are. Keep that in mind when reading its position in the chart.

Sign Venus is in Scorpio (transformative, intense, deep), therefore Venus is filtered through the qualities of Scorpio. Through the filter of Scorpio's traits, Claire is loyal, seeks loyalty, depth and intimacy. She seeks feeling and requires the same in return. She also looks for transformation in her relationships.

Element Scorpio is Water element (emotional, sensitive). This means Claire relates through emotional connection. She needs to feel that unspoken bond, is receptive to non-verbal cues and will look for emotional security and stability. She'll be caring and seek to merge with her loves, friends and desires.

Mode Scorpio is Fixed mode (determined, constant). The Fixed mode means Claire doesn't let go of her desires easily and will focus in on what she wants.

House Venus in the 6th House (daily work, service, routine and health). Libra (balance, harmony) is on the cusp of the 6th House. With Claire's Venus in the 6th House, it tells us that she will express the qualities of Venus as part of her work. And that she'll need routines that are Venusian to maintain a balance in her health. Claire is a make-up artist (so she transforms others), as well as a singer-songwriter (she channels passion), both careers allow Claire to express her Venus. Libra is on the cusp of the 6th House, meaning harmony and beauty are a vital part of maintaining mind/body health. Balance is essential. If there is discord at work or daily, Claire's health will suffer. Libra is an Air sign, so connection with others is also essential on a daily basis.

Aspects Venus sextile Mercury, Venus square Uranus. Mercury is 60° away from Venus which makes the Sextile aspect – a very easy and fruitful aspect. This means the function of Mercury and Venus operate well together, with a little zest and not much effort. Claire can express her love and desires with charm and ease. And she has a creative style of communication, ideal for a singer/songwriter.

Uranus is 90° from Venus, forming a Square aspect. Squares are challenging aspects, which means the more challenging Uranus traits will be pitted against the Venus function. Uranus is rebellious, ahead of its time, a changemaker and disruptive. With Venus, these qualities will inform Claire's style of relating, beauty ideals and what she finds attractive. She may react suddenly rather than smoothly and relationships could begin unexpectedly as well as end abruptly.

I. Planets

Planets are a fundamental part of reading a birth chart. They represent various archetypal aspects of our psyche and selves. Each planet, like an actor or character, has a particular role to play and function to express. For example, the Moon represents our emotions and Venus represents love. Knowing the role each planet plays in your life is vital to understanding astrology.

Get to know the keywords for each planet and its function. This will help you read what is happening in your birth chart. Think of planets as the 'what' – what is being expressed. Later, you'll see that the signs are the 'how' – how that function of the planet is being expressed. And the houses are the 'where', in what area of life – from career to home – this expression is taking place.

The way we express the function of the planets, and in what area of life we do it, helps us understand our needs at any time. If, for example, you are on a date and expressing your Venus, you might also express your Mars (the planet of action) when you decide it's time to call it a night, or even make a romantic move. Or if you are upset and emotional, you will be expressing your emotions in keeping with your Moon. Knowing the needs of that particular Moon is a shortcut to understanding yourself. So understanding how and where the planets express their unique functions is key to everything.

Keep it personal: Sun, Moon, Mercury, Venus and Mars

The inner planets that are closest to the Sun are our personal planets – these include the Sun, as well as the Moon, Mercury, Venus and Mars. These orbit the Sun faster than the outer planets and tend to impact our day-to-day lives. They represent fast-moving, personal functions, including the self, communication, emotions, actions and love. Basically all of our daily concerns. Meanwhile, the outer planets have longer orbital times, and impact other parts of our lives, such as change and responsibility.

Focus on the inner planets first before graduating to the outer planets. They reveal the most about you and others. Give them more weight when reading your birth chart.

Find harmony: Saturn and Jupiter

Outer planets Saturn and Jupiter describe two opposing areas of life that need equal harmony in order to maintain balance – it's useful to read both planets together in order to fully understand them and their impact. Together they're our social and cultural connections. Saturn represents our limitations, fears and what we need to master. Jupiter suggests where we have faith, luck and natural abundance. Jupiter is our inner guru that encourages us to follow our bliss. These two planets were the final two in traditional astrology for thousands of years. Until only a few hundred years ago, they represented the limits of our Universe, life, and consciousness.

The wounded healer: Chiron

Chiron is an asteroid and known as the shaman of the Universe. It's an addition to the ten standard planets modern astrologers refer to and was discovered in 1977. It is associated with healing, so mastering Chiron in our chart lays the foundation for achieving higher levels of wholeness and happiness, and for finding our inner mystical potential.

Take a trip: Uranus, Neptune, Pluto

These three planets are slow moving with long orbital times, therefore they represent universal themes and trends that mark each passing generation. Their energies are high voltage and thoroughly transformative. They can be complex or esoteric to understand, but there is a mystical level to our world and our abilities, so it's worth tapping into their functions. Work into these slowly, with intent and an open mind. They represent divine doorways, so be ready to engage your intuitive mind with them and look for how you can best express them in a positive way to power up your inner mystic.

Planets ruling signs

Each planet is associated with one or two signs that share their flavour, yet have different functions. The planet is called the sign ruler – it's 'ruling' that sign. For example, Mars (action) rules Aries (independence) – so if your birth chart shows Mars in Aries, you'll be easily assertive and driven. In these cases, the function of the planet is at its peak.

Check the chart on the inside cover of this book to see which sign each planet is ruled by.

Rising planets

The planets in the 1st House are known as the rising planets. Together with the personal planets, you should give these planets a little more attention when reading your birth chart.

Sun
Get your shine on

Sense of self · Self-expression · Identity
Personality · Vitality · Power · Direction

RULES Leo
RULES 5th House
RULES heart, solar plexus and thymus gland
ASTROLOGICAL ORBITAL TIME 1 year
TRANSITS EACH ZODIAC SIGN 1 month
STRONG in Aries and Leo
NEEDS CONSCIOUS EFFORT in Libra, Aquarius and Pisces

The Sun is the star of the show in our solar system, the undisputed ruler around which all other celestial bodies rotate. Its magnetic pull commands the orbit of every other planet in its entourage. It's the centring and creative force for our home, planet Earth.

Worshipped over millennia as the supreme deity, it has had entire religions devoted to it. It could fit 1.3 million Earths into its colossal heavenly body. No wonder it represents our ego!

We're all here to get our shine on, and that is the role of the Sun in our chart. It represents our individual life force, our will to live, our purpose, our direction and our conscious self-awareness. The question 'who am I?' is answered by the Sun's placement within each sign, house and aspect in a birth chart.

The Sun is the part of you that is boss, the CEO, top of the pile. The Sun is all about the business of being you. It helps you express yourself authentically, to learn about yourself and to develop your sense of self. The Sun represents our own personal light. How well we can hold our own light and shine depends on a healthy sense of self. When we're in harmony, we have a healthy ego: we can stand in our sense of self without projecting our own positive or negative qualities onto others.

The glyph for the Sun in astrology is a circle with a small dot at the centre. The central dot symbolises the focused awareness of our consciousness, the larger circle denotes our limitless and unrealised potential. The goal of a lifetime is to integrate all parts of ourselves into consciousness, accepting ourselves for who we truly are. Peak experience comes when we strike harmony between the boundary of our everyday identity and our expanded state of awareness represented by the dot and the circle. This is the ultimate goal of both ancient and modern mystics.

Expressing your Sun in the positive

You appreciate others' self-expression and create win-win mutual appreciation relationships with ease. Feeling ignited, recharged and inspired by others, you are their equal. You have a healthy sense of empathy and concern for others while maintaining a stable base for yourself and your own needs.

Look to express your purpose and follow your passion – it will light you up and energise you. Step into the light, take responsibility for yourself and shine bright.

If anyone has a beef with your self-expression, it could be their own issues, not yours. Refuse to be told to get back in your lane and don't accept external or internalised limiting voices saying 'should not', 'do not' or 'no'. You have the potential to light the path for yourself and others. Listen for and stay true to your inner light, your inner 'yes', your inner Sun.

Expressing your Sun in the negative

Losing sight of a healthy ego can lead to an overinflated sense of self. Egotistical, egocentric and narcissistic tendencies of being overly concerned with oneself, lack of empathy for others and a sense of entitlement turn others off supporting your shine. Not that you care.

Equal relationships can't be formed since you see others as existing entirely to serve or praise numero uno. Demands for VIP treatment eventually fall on deaf ears as an overriding self-interest drives others away.

If you're overcompensating for a weak sense of self or ego, a grandiose sense of entitlement and self-importance will leave you threatened by others' confidence and ability to express themselves. If you feel like you need to dominate and control others, your image and situations you're in, your vital energy and potential will be frittered away.

Playing down your own light diminishes your vital life force, plus projecting your needs onto someone else and expecting them to shine for you also diminishes a central part of yourself. By not allowing yourself to live authentically, you can experience low energy, burnout and unrealised potential and dreams.

A weakened or diminished sense of self means less radiance, health, happiness and personal fulfilment. You allow yourself to become a doormat by not standing up for yourself or your needs. You don't have a connection to who you really are, therefore lack direction, traction and confidence. You may blame others for your problems as you don't recognise your own ability to actualise your dreams. Giving your power away invites others to take advantage of you and at worst exposes you to abuse. If you don't respect your life force, or assert yourself or your boundaries, no one else will.

Your inner mystic will enjoy a lack of ego, yet your ego is necessary for survival in a material world. It's like an operating system for everyday life, and it's vital to return to it after experiencing oneness or other forays 'beyond self'. Lack of self may result in being overwhelmed by others' personalities and taking on problems that simply aren't yours. It's just not worth it. The life of our Sun's ballast on Earth is finite, so make the most of it. You only live this life once – be who you want to be remembered for. You do you.

The Sun in your birth chart

The Sun in a sign
The sign the Sun is in indicates your style of self-expression, identity, potential and your life force. This is your 'star' sign!

Taurus · As an Earth sign, you tend to bring the strength of the material plane to your solar principle – you're shining in a material world after all! You radiate a solid, earthy vibe and have constancy.

Pisces · Oriented toward sensitivity, subtlety and selflessness. You need to balance your love of transcending the material realm with a strong sense of self-identity. Your energy is often gentle as well as playful.

Scorpio · Survival mode is staying hidden, while the Sun is meant to shine out loud and proud. You can often be found as the real power behind the throne. You tend to radiate a magnetic vibe.

The Sun in a house

The house the Sun occupies in your birth chart is the area of life where you shine, learn about yourself and develop a sense of self.

10th House · You shine in your career and public image. Reputation is everything. You'll need to be autonomous if working for others, but with your name on the door you'll have leadership potential. You may be well suited to running your own business. You were built for empire. You'll learn about and develop your self through work, recognition and achievement outside of the home. Career is an imperative.

12th House · Requires plenty of alone time to connect in, centre and recharge. There's a strong need for escapism, so find healthy ways of expressing an expanded sense of self. Choose the path of the mystic or the actor, or other avenues that express your compassion satisfyingly. You naturally pick up on collective ideas and consciousness. You shine in selfless, humble pursuits, while your downfall will be your ego.

The Sun in aspect to another planet

In aspect to another planet, the Sun contributes with energy and consciousness to how that planet functions. The other planet(s) involved colour our identity and the way we express who we are.

Mercury · Identity is easily expressed through communication. You talk a lot and shine when sharing creative ideas. A sunny mindset.

Neptune · Sensitive, empathetic and compassionate. Energy is charged by artistic pursuits. You identify with the path of the mystic and pick up on vibrations from the environment. You need to learn to work with sensitivity as a gift, or it can bring confusion.

How to tap your inner Sun

Power pose · To amp up your light charge, boost your confidence and lower stress ahead of a meeting or exam, give this a go. Stand in a power pose like Wonder Woman, hands on hips or arms stretched up and out, legs strong, feet apart like a star. Hold for two minutes. Visualise yourself accomplishing your intention, expand the growth feelings in your body.

Take up more space in the room by physically expressing open postures so your natural pharmacy kicks in. Why minimise your Sun (self) by closing down your body? Taking up less space turns your light's dimmer switch down. What would a queen of the jungle do? Same as the queen of the boardroom. Own it!

Thymus thump · To add a further boost, beat your chest like King Kong. The thymus thump helps release energy, power you up and create a shield and force that tells others who's coming.

Own your traits · Owning all of our traits is key to authenticity and personal power. Projecting either our best traits onto others and creating a fantasy character, or alternatively casting our unwanted traits onto others, disempowers us. We've all been there. When you suspect you're doing either of those things, try this exercise.

Write down all those positive traits that draw you in to the person you might be casting your light onto. List where you exhibit these qualities in your own life, as well as who has recognised each trait in you. It's a great way to reclaim your shine.

You can do the same for projected negative traits: list the traits you dislike about the person, or those that trigger a negative response. Then write down where you have exhibited these traits in your life. Next, write down how these traits have actually been of benefit and service to you. The point is to integrate all your myriad facets to harness the full potential of your Sun. Level up and own up. Integration is the key to working your solar power to the maximum.

Moon
Your inner sanctum

Emotional nature · Feelings · Changeability
Nurture · Security · Safety · Instincts

RULES Cancer
RULES 4th House
RULES breasts and lymphatic system
ASTROLOGICAL ORBITAL TIME 28 days
TRANSITS EACH ZODIAC SIGN 2.3 days
STRONG in Cancer and Taurus
NEEDS CONSCIOUS EFFORT in Scorpio and Capricorn

The Moon is technically a satellite rather than a planet. Along with the Sun, it's termed a 'luminary'. With the fastest orbit cycle in the zodiac, 27.3 days, the Moon is seen as changeable, as are our emotions. From the tides of Earth to our bodies' monthly cycle, we're locked into its rhythm of waxing and waning light, as well as the gravitational pull of its orbit.

While the part of ourselves indicated by the Sun's placement may be obvious, the Moon is hidden from view. Our inner sanctum, as represented by the Moon, reveals our instinctual and emotional disposition or nature. This is our feeling function. It's often unconscious and coloured by our early childhood experiences and memories.

When you're all about the feelings, you're functioning from the part of yourself represented by the Moon. Understanding the condition of the Moon in your chart will tell you all about your emotional needs: what makes you feel nurtured, safe and secure. To engage another person emotionally, look at the sign and placement of their Moon.

In Vedic (Indian) astrology, the Moon is considered more important than the Sun in a chart as we are born with the Moon part of ourselves at full strength, while the Sun is developed over time. The Moon is less obvious, but don't underestimate the nature it represents in either yourself or others.

As our emotions are connected to memories that seem to blend and merge like pools of water, they can colour isolated current events and perspectives. This is why emotional reactions can seem out of proportion to an event. Our Moon is there to protect and keep us safe, nourished, sheltered and loved. It represents an essential yet primal part of ourselves that is always switched on and scanning our environment. An overreaction is often linked to an overblown perceived threat to our survival. Our ability to be low-stress-reactive can determine our success in the world – harness your feelings to inform rather than drive you.

Our own self-reflection, mindfulness and introspection can build emotional intelligence (EQ), to balance basic needs with our function as rational adults. As an incentive, it's worth knowing that the best CEOs tend not to have the highest IQs, they have high EQs. Accept your emotions and work your Moon, or as with all planets, it'll trip you up from the shadows.

Expressing your Moon in the positive

You are in touch with your emotions and comfortable with your feelings. You have a good handle on self-care as well as caring for and connecting emotionally with others. You know what you need to feel safe and make healthy emotional decisions. You have a healthy relationship with food and you like nourishing others. Your gut instincts are accurate and you easily hear and follow this inner knowledge. You feel secure in your relationships, you're open-hearted and you love with ease.

Expressing your Moon in the negative

You either suppress your emotions or underperform in self-care. You may resent others when they express their emotional needs because you're afraid to express your own. Needy people trigger you, causing you to shut down emotionally. Or, you may be the needy one who never feels satisfied or you think that you don't receive enough love. You find it hard to open your heart to giving or receiving love. You don't trust your body's natural instinctual needs or knowledge, denying a valuable source of information about your environment.

The Moon in your birth chart

The Moon in a sign
The sign the Moon is in indicates what you need to feel emotionally safe, secure and nourished. It describes the nature of your emotional self.

Taurus · You are slow to anger, but if the bull begins to rage, you have a tendency to open the fridge and pile all your favourites on a plate. Quality food and drink helps everything. The Moon is 'exalted' in Taurus, which makes you reliable and emotionally consistent. It can be hard for you to move on if a relationship is over.

Leo · You have a natural flair for the dramatic. Often colourful and creative, you can be the life and soul of the party. Tantrums can be Oscar-worthy, but tomorrow is a new day with no grudges held. Leo Moon is fun! And creative. Make sure you have an outlet for creative expression, even if it's having great hair and fabulous frocks. Leo Moons need to be noticed and admired. If you know one, take them out to play often and express how you feel about them regularly. Say it with grand statements so they know they're both safe and adored.

The Moon in a house
The house the Moon occupies in your birth chart is the area of life where we seek nurture, benefit from natural gut instincts and tend to express ourselves emotionally. This area of life can be changeable and involve women in some way.

2nd House · You'll have a canny knack for knowing how and when to cash in those shares and make bank. Emotional life and family are valued. You'll make a living through your caring and nurturing capacity, which could involve the food industry.

10th House · You have a gut instinct for what the public wants; you'll connect emotionally through career and public image.

11th House · Friends and groups become like family. Groups and acquaintances will tend to be female or have a focus on emotional life. You have a natural instinct for social trends as well as an urge toward humanitarian social responsibility, particularly around women's issues or caring for others.

The Moon in aspect to another planet

In aspect to another planet, the Moon brings feeling and gut instinct to how that planet functions. The planet(s) aspecting the Moon in your birth chart help describe our style of connecting and emotional needs.

Mercury · Communication will be emotive and feelings will be subjects for discussion. Talking about feelings provides emotional connection.

Mars · This combo produces an emotional warrior. Emotional energy is assertive. There is a drive to connect emotionally.

How to tap your inner Moon

Moonbeams are more delicate than the Sun's blazing rays, so approaching from a quiet place or indirectly is helpful. If upset or unsure about an issue, use this technique to get closer to it, open it up and bring clarity.

Close your eyes, drop into your body and become aware of your internal state. Use your senses. Just sit and notice what comes up when you think about the situation. Notice if there's a colour, an image… Is there a texture? If it's in an area of your body, how much space does it occupy? Are there any words or sounds? Ask if it's OK to sit with it, to keep it company.

Continue in this vein as the senses and imagery soften and open up. Never force, push or demand. Building up trust with your inner self is important for this receptive part. This gentle technique can be used solo, or with a friend or partner.

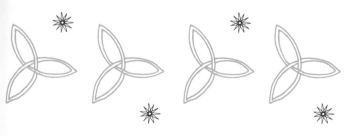

Mercury
Telling it like it is

**Curiosity · Restlessness · Intellect · Communication
Learning · Connection · Trickster**

RULES Gemini and Virgo
RULES 3rd and 6th House
RULES nervous system and lungs
ASTROLOGICAL ORBITAL TIME approximately 1 year
TRANSITS EACH ZODIAC SIGN approximately 1 month
STRONG in Gemini, Virgo and Aquarius
NEEDS CONSCIOUS EFFORT in Sagittarius, Leo and Pisces

First planet out from the Sun, Mercury is the fastest-orbiting in our Solar System. Taking roughly one year to make a return, Mercury keeps pace with Earth's orbit. Therefore it'll be found in the same sign or one away from your Sun sign. As the Sun's closest confidant, it helps us identify with our thoughts, ideas and beliefs.

Mercury represents our minds. Our communication style, ability to think and reason, whether we prefer Snapchat or long-form non-fiction – all are indicated by Mercury. This is our thinking and reasoning function.

Named after the Roman messenger of the gods, Mercury can be a fast-talking street hustler one minute, or a sophisticated socialite the next. This part of us is quick, restless and impartial, and can move through all spheres of thought. It links all areas of the mind: left and right hemispheres, conscious and unconscious. The glyph shows the circle of spirit or source of energy connecting both the cross of matter and the higher mind or soul. In mythology, Mercury is the only one who can freely travel between worlds. Ultimately our minds have the same potential.

Mercury is best used when given freedom to be curious, explore and expand our world. A free, open mind is a free, open world.

Expressing Mercury in the positive

You're direct in communicating ideas, and you can listen to others and engage people in conversation. You have a great attention span and have no trouble switching off your mind when it's time to rest and subdue your inner critic. You are curious about new ideas and don't identify with old, internalised ideas you've outgrown. You understand the mind/body connection and how thoughts affect physical chemistry, so you make healthy choices on perspectives and where to focus your attention. You've harnessed the power of your mind to support living the life you love.

Expressing Mercury in the negative

Your inner critic is running the show, and you find it hard to switch off the chatter in your mind when it's time to rest or sleep. You're preoccupied and not able to ground your attention in the present moment. You're lost in your mind: your thoughts are confused and you find it difficult to connect through communication with others. You identify with your negative notions, giving them further power over your mind, perspective, beliefs, actions and life.

Mercury in your birth chart

Mercury in a sign
The sign Mercury is in indicates what condition your mind is in, and the style of communication and learning you require. It also reveals what catches our ear and piques our intellectual interest. Do you prefer a one-liner or an hour of monologue?

Sagittarius · An accent will cause you to prick up your ears, you'll be great at seeing the connections between diverse areas, and you'll be naturally philosophical. Queen of the turnaround, you can find a silver lining in the darkest cloud. If others don't laugh at your jokes, you certainly will. You're an upbeat communicator and an avid learner and teacher. Thanks to the Sagittarian principle of expansion, you tend to need too much information before moving forward.

Pisces · You pick up on what people really mean – their non-verbals leave an impression on you. You often have a dreamy, creative mind that recalls events visually. This is a great placement for poetry, writing music or anything requiring a brain that needs to make serious creative leaps.

Mercury in a house
The house Mercury occupies in your chart is the zone where we communicate and learn. This area of life is of great interest so we tend to share ideas here.

1st House · You want to talk to everyone you meet; you'll be great in sales and have a curious, communicative outlook.

2nd House · You'll have plenty of ideas on how to grow the bottom line, and enjoy thinking about values and things of value. Income is connected to communication and bright ideas.

5th House · Mercury in the 5th House brings creative expression, particularly in writing or communication. Dates will only pass muster if they're intellectually stimulating and full of fun facts. The silent type won't make it to a second date! There'll be plenty of plans for fun and you find games stimulating.

Mercury in aspect to another planet
In aspect to another planet Mercury contributes curiosity, a quickness of pace and comprehension to how that planet functions. The other planet will influence Mercury's interest and function in terms of learning, processing logic and communications.

Venus · Mercury in aspect to Venus loves to read, write, talk, think and communicate, and *really* loves the sound of their own voice! They have lyrical, charming speech with a talent for creative writing and the language of love. They'll value communication, ideas and artistic pursuits, but may also spend time thinking about how to relate, and make connections and money. They like to keep speech convivial.

Pluto · This brings the power of the mind, communication and transformative words. What's more, it brings the detective mind: a deeply penetrating quality that tends to search out the hidden aspects of life. You may pick up on knowledge in a way that almost seems psychic to others. You'll be a deep thinker with little interest in small talk, instead using a powerfully magnetic communication style. Watch out for obsessive thoughts!

How to tap your inner Mercury

Our mind can drift back to the past (depression), or rest too much in the future (anxiety). Reflection and planning are important, but the present moment is the eye of the needle, the only real point from which creative change can be made. In this age of ever-growing distraction designed to attract your attention, mindfulness can be used to reclaim this precious resource. By focusing your awareness on things that exist only in the moment, on what you're doing right now or on your own bodily sensations, you can easily anchor your mind in the present.

Try doing a body scan, from the top of your head all the way down to your toes every time you need to bring your mind back and 'ground' it. With practice, this basic technique gives us control over our minds, as well as more objectivity in immediate situations.

Or sit quietly, eyes closed, and begin to notice your thoughts. Without judging them, allow thoughts to come up naturally then let them go without pursuing them. Practise detaching yourself from them. Watch them as if they're on a screen. If you find yourself attaching to them and being drawn in, return to your breath and go back to watching them impartially.

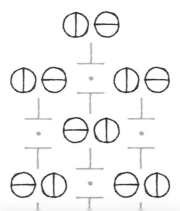

♀ Venus
Life's sweetest reward

Love · Desire · Relationships · Values · Style
Aesthetics · Beauty · Money · Social factor

RULES Taurus and Libra
RULES 2nd and 7th House
RULES symmetry and beauty
ASTROLOGICAL ORBITAL TIME 1 year
TRANSITS EACH ZODIAC SIGN approximately 1 month
STRONG in Taurus, Libra and Pisces
NEEDS CONSCIOUS EFFORT in Aries, Virgo and Scorpio

Venus appears as the morning star, and at the opposite phase of its cycle, the evening star. Second from the Sun, it's the third-brightest celestial body after the Sun and the Moon.

If Venus in your birth chart is positioned ahead of your Sun, you have the morning star vibe, after the Sun and you're an evening star. As the morning star it was known as an active-energy warrior queen, the Roman goddess of sexuality and fertility. It was known in pre-Biblical times by the name Lucifer, the light-bearer. Those born with Venus in its morning star phase will be dynamic and passionate in ardour, diving in headfirst, while those in the evening star phase are more receptive and mature.

Hey, lovers! Venus represents how, where and with whom we get amorous. It controls our desire and our love style. Venus is the doyenne at the door with the clipboard list of who's worth being let in and who has to stand out in the rain. The list is comparative to our own sense of self-worth. How do you rate your own value? Highly, that's right!

Venus is the part of you that wants relationships. Relationships of all kinds. It's our personal brand of social lubricant. It's all about how you relate (sign and aspect), where you like to relate (house) and with whom.

Our charm, flirt style, aesthetics and even decorating style are largely informed by the sign and house placement of Venus.

Check your Venus placements if ever in doubt of compatibility with another person. Combined with the Moon, these two planets are incredibly useful in determining relationship compatibility when comparing two charts. A tick from both gets you past go. Also, look specifically at the aspects in your charts – you'll learn more about this later in the book. But note your Venus conjunct or trine a partner's Moon, Sun or Venus is a great start. You will feel (Moon) loved (Venus) by them. Square aspects are tense and you really do have different love styles – it will take work, and you should only proceed if you have other favourable connections to lean on when gears start to grind.

Expressing Venus in the positive

Because you know your worth, and you value yourself, you know how to have your needs met in a win-win way. You are attracted to people who collaborate, and accept, love and commit.

You are friendly, sociable and charming, able to meet new people as well as maintain relationships. Your ability to see the beauty and connect on a loving, sociable level with all types of people creates a positive feedback loop.

You know what you love and desire, so you are authentic in how you relate to others. Therefore the relationships you surround yourself with are rewarding and you feel loved. Your choices are in alignment with your values.

You have an appreciation for beauty and the arts, while also having your own personal style. Self care and pampering come easily. Venus represents the goddess archetype and you're comfortable with expressing your own version.

Because you are clear on your values, you are able to pin your income and spending to what you value the most. This keeps up your motivation and earning potential. When spending money you express gratitude for what your dollar buys, therefore the river of abundance flows to you.

Expressing Venus in the negative

Venus is all about love and relating, so a negative expression will be too 'me, me, me'. Social skills may be lacking, leaving you as the ultimate wallflower. You may be clingy, possessive, jealous or even suspicious, especially if you've put all your eggs in one basket. On the other end of the scale, commitment could be a problem, as could being too detached or fearful of becoming intimate. If you don't value yourself you may not have the discernment you need to form healthy relationships or friendships may be detrimental to you.

If self-worth is low, then social and relationship problems, as well as personal and financial ones, could be an issue. You may not make the most of your beauty, preferring to play it down. In polarity you could be vain, giving too much sway to social appearance or status rather than authentic personal connection.

Venus in your birth chart

Venus in a sign
The sign Venus is in indicates what type of relationship you desire. It also reveals what motivates you to form relationships. What's your love style, are you a lover or a fighter? The sign indicates what we value.

Aries · Venus through the direct filter of Aries won't leave you guessing. You are the cavewoman of the zodiac: you know what you want and will let people around you know.

Virgo · Venus needs a little extra conscious effort here as you can become critical of those you love (you expect perfection!). You show your love by picking up on what people need and providing it.

Libra · In rulership, Libra Venus lends natural charm and an easy sense of style. You love and need beauty in your life and have a great appreciation for the finer things. You love to love.

Pisces · Pisces is known to have soft boundaries: Venus here loves everyone, functioning well in this sensitive and open sign.

Venus in a house
The house Venus occupies in your birth chart is the area of life where you seek to relate and form relationships. This area of life will be high on your list of values and may indicate a source of income.

4th House · You need a beautiful home and tend to entertain from its comfort. You may make money from your home base. You tend to love family and have positive regard for your upbringing and memories.

7th House · You love to relate one-on-one. As the marrying type, you prefer charming, good-looking partners and tend to attract wealth through coupling up.

11th House · You're a party girl who loves a social scene. You enjoy relating to new people and finding common interests.

Venus in aspect to another planet

In aspect to another planet, Venus contributes charm, beauty and harmony to how that planet functions. It adds an extra dimension to both your love style and how you relate to others.

Sun · Venus brings charm and diplomacy to expressing yourself. You identify with beauty and often have a feminine overlay to your look and personality. You light up when relating to others and may live for love. You value personality and may make money by amplifying your own.

Uranus · Venus picks up all sorts of quirks and unusual ways of relating from Uranus. You'll be interested in anyone who seems different from the status quo and you'll enjoy relating to all sorts of people. Your love life may be a little unusual and you may have a preference for independence and space. Your beauty ideals tilt toward eccentric, cutting-edge or all-out Age-of-Aquarius hippie style. Your income may be influenced by using technology or new methods.

How to tap your inner Venus

Look for the beauty and harmony around you in nature, in individuals and even interactions. By seeing the beauty in all things, you'll develop your Venusian capacity.

Mars
Just do it!

**Impulsiveness · Dynamism · Assertiveness
Action · Willpower · Warrior**

RULES Aries
RULES 1st House
RULES adrenals
ASTROLOGICAL ORBITAL TIME 2 years
TRANSITS EACH ZODIAC SIGN approximately 2 months
STRONG in Aries, Scorpio and Capricorn
NEEDS CONSCIOUS EFFORT in Libra, Taurus and Cancer

Fourth from the Sun, Mars may be visible to the naked eye with its fiery red colour, but its temps are 80 below zero. The planet representing action invites a lot of activity – it has been the subject of more space missions, both completed and planned, than any other.

The glyph for Mars is the circle of spirit topped by an arrow pointing outward and upward. The part of us that's built to go get it needs external expression, up and out. As the co-pilot to the Sun, Mars is how we get the job done.

It's with Mars that we get up in the grill of the world and assert ourselves. When we have a plan (Mercury) and know what we want (Venus), it's Mars that takes action.

Mars is the initial responder. Without activating our Mars by acting on our ideas, needs, wants, inspirations, dreams, intuition, emotions and desires, our energy can become frustrated and turn inward. Think of any two-year-old child: well, Mars is like that. It takes two years to orbit. When it returns to its placement in the birth chart it's appropriately known as the 'terrible twos'. Emotions bottled up can explode in red-hot outbursts of fury, which when turned inward, can affect our health.

Want to change the world or get where you want to go? Work your Mars. Get behind the wheel in 100% of your life, put your foot on the accelerator then steer your own course.

The moment is missed if you repress your impulse to act. When a wave comes in, it's wise to move at the right time to catch it. Your impulse to action can be like that. You have your own innate timing and intuition. Unexpressed, Mars energy is diffused, misdirected or internalised indirectly. Think about the frustration you may have experienced when you know you should have acted on something and didn't, because you hesitated, doubted yourself or listened to someone else instead of your own wisdom.

Culturally both the Sun and Mars have been presented as overtly male archetypes. However, like the Sun, Mars is an archetype representing a necessary function we all have to survive and thrive regardless of gender. Females in most modern cultures are generally brought up to repress their active, assertive, aggressive and self-interested side: we're encouraged to give it away to others. We're socialised to repress this powerful function while setting a 'desirable' standard for attractiveness as pleasing, passive and dependant.

Women have extra work to do when it comes to moving beyond limiting and narrow cultural codes of 'acceptable' and 'attractive' behaviour in order to unleash our full potential in this world. Just being aware of this helps us begin to notice when you're holding yourself back, or when others are doing it to you. Support your own actions and surround yourself with people who also support them.

Expressing Mars in the positive

When you feel that initial impulse to act, you can follow it easily and get into a flow. If others impede your progress in reaching your dreams, or following your own inner drive, you push on regardless. You take responsibility for getting what you want and where you want – you trust the wisdom of your inner mystic and set about delivering tangible results in the real world. Your plans could be concrete and realistic, or they could be vague – either way, you just 'know' and go. When you follow your inner compass, you feel satisfied, energised and empowered.

Expressing Mars in the negative

Not acting in response to a toxic situation results in adrenals constantly firing. Think of a car with its pedal to the metal, but it's chained by its towbar. There'll be wear and tear, probably some kind of burnout. Ill health and fatigue is the result, further weakening the ability to mobilise.

The 'damsel in distress' fairytales are classic illustrations of women giving away the Mars principle. When you project your Mars onto someone else, expecting them to do for you, save you, make your dreams come true or get you what/where you want, you are effectively giving away your power to actualise the very circumstance you want. Boring. Giving away your power to protect yourself, leaving you vulnerable and dependant? Still boring. It's like putting someone else behind the wheel. You can only go where they take you, which is often where they want to go! Mars in Aries is unlikely to stay in a situation like this, but Mars in Pisces probably will.

Mars in your birth chart

Mars in a sign
The sign Mars is in indicates what flavour of action and assertion you require. It also reveals what motivates us into action. Are you a lover or a fighter?

Leo · You take dramatic action: slammed doors and walk-outs ensure things will change.

Cancer · You move to protect and secure, so cuddle time on the couch with a movie and popcorn is essential. Never underestimate the power of food to motivate you!

Capricorn · Often in the charts of successful people. You love practical action and thrive on grit and hard work, creating a path to the top. While others sleep, you're driving through the night.

Pisces · Gentle and indirect, but you can also be passive-aggressive. This Mars functions best in roles requiring creativity or sensitivity. Meditation, soaking in water or getting lost in a movie are good ways to re-energise.

Mars in a house

The house Mars occupies in our natal chart is the action zone where we strike out, assert ourselves and need to let off steam. It also indicates where we can recharge ourselves.

1st House · A great placement for roles requiring assertiveness.

9th House · You'll need to roam far and wide. You could be ambitious academically, or perhaps have energy and drive to build a media empire. Travel, study and philosophising will build your energy reserves.

4th House · You have plenty of energy for working on the house; a home gym would be suitable too, depending on the sign. You'll be assertive and independent, and know how you want everything done. Mars rules sharp metal objects, so you may even decorate with these or practise martial arts using weapons at home.

Mars in aspect to another planet

In aspect to another planet, Mars contributes energy, assertion and drive to how that planet functions.

Mercury · A great combo for debating... or arguing. There will be forceful, assertive speech that may tip into angry or aggressive, a racing or fast mind that thinks on the go.

Venus · Assertive in love and making connections. You prefer bold aesthetics. Strong in sales and useful in making money by being direct and active.

How to tap your inner Mars

Practice following up the impulse to act that you feel in your body with tangible action. Make sure its an upward expansive feeling – that's the positive one. When you move in flow with your instincts and desires, you'll find you move in flow with the Universe. This is when the magic happens!

♃ Jupiter
Going supernova

Expansion · Growth · Faith · Optimism
Abundance · Generosity · Luck

RULES Sagittarius
RULES 9ᵗʰ House
RULES liver, pituitary gland and growth
ASTROLOGICAL ORBITAL TIME 12 years
TRANSITS EACH ZODIAC SIGN 1 year
STRONG in Cancer, Sagittarius and Pisces
NEEDS CONSCIOUS EFFORT in Capricorn, Gemini and Virgo

Jupiter is the size-queen of our interstellar planetary line-up. Sporting 67 plus moons, this massive, gaseous planet dwarfs everything in our solar system except the Sun. Themes of expansion and largesse are key to reading the Jupiter effect. Fifth from the Sun, Jupiter is jacked up on helium, expressing the natural buoyancy it injects into life. The planet even has a bulge at its equator… typical Jupiter excess!

Walk into a room like you own it and you probably will end up doing just that. Jupiter represents the power of positivity and the absolute faith that the Universe has our back. Confidence trumps competence. With that in mind, we throw caution to the wind as we take risks that lead to expansion and growth.

Attuned to opportunity, Jupiter seizes the day. We all have an area in our life where we're excited about the prospect of turning lemons into lemonade. Jupiter doesn't see the glass half-empty, it sees it half-full and ready to be filled even more.

In Roman mythology Jupiter (aka Zeus in Greek mythology) was in charge, dishing out gifts and favours as well as making final judgments. Jupiter helps us think big and bold. In the face of failure, it'll opt for next level rather than settle.

As queen of the turnaround, it'll take its best shot and transform failure into a great piece of fortune. This is the lucky planet. When we stride through life with belief in a positive outcome, generosity, honesty and an open heart, we're far more likely to succeed.

In Vedic (Indian) astrology, Jupiter is called the guru, the teacher – it's the dispeller of darkness (ignorance) through knowledge. Lessons learned from mistakes are gathered and used to our advantage in the next round, and the practice of gratitude lets our higher mind deliver more of what we say 'yes' to. The getting of wisdom then returning the favour by teaching others from a spirit of generosity is part of Jupiter's two-way street.

Overdoing your Jupiter

You can have too much of a good thing. Jupiter is the planet of overdoing it all, which can have its pitfalls. Its dark side is full of hot air, empty promises and overextension. Excess can show up as a lack of boundaries and an unrealistic outlook, making us take risks and gamble. You might be unrealistic, preachy and judgmental, or be prone to overreaching and excess.

The antidote
The planet following Jupiter is Saturn, which can help modify any Jupiter excess. Work with the Jupiter principles of faith, expansion and risk-taking, but for balance, maintain Saturn principles of containment through limits, responsibility and realistic expectations.

Underdoing your Jupiter

If Jupiter's buoyancy is restrained you can lose your connection to society, leaving you isolated. Lack of meaning and understanding of the larger picture breeds fear of stepping out of the safe lane.

You might find yourself elevating and worshipping modern celebrities to the status of gurus – it takes the place of looking within for answers, which ultimately is where you'll find Jupiter's wisdom.

The antidote

Identify where you've been limiting and restricting yourself and how you can open those areas up. Practise letting go and repeat positive affirmations, backed up with noting as many personal positives as negatives.

Confidence-enhancing exercises build up your sense of self. Work your Jupiter by helping others who need it, so you get out into a new area, as well as seeing your own fortune compared to others. Challenge yourself by joining a team sports group or taking a class in something you've always wanted to try.

Jupiter in your chart

Jupiter in a sign

The sign Jupiter is in indicates what kind of luck you possess, what flavour your faith is and what you seek to bring meaning into your life.

Leo · With confidence in self-expression, you'll find that luck and opportunity meet when you let yourself be you. Your hair will be a talking point and you'll naturally fall into leadership positions. You know how to mark an occasion by celebrating with drama and opulence.

Scorpio · Jupiter's buoyancy brings light to life's depths and mysteries. You'll have luck in shared enterprise and confidence tackling hidden aspects or taboo areas of life. You'll seek out esoteric teachings and the metaphysical side of reality. You're a confident manifester. Lucky and confident in intimacy, you learn from your deep bonds with others.

Jupiter in a house

The house Jupiter occupies in your birth chart reveals the area of life where you have some luck waiting for you. It's also where you seek situations that will expand your experience, mind and understanding, as well as your place in society. You'll seek a higher meaning in this area of life.

1st House · This placement bestows a positive outlook and ability to spot a new opportunity quickly. Popularity is a given as you easily inspire good feelings in others. Watch the waistline, as it'll be hard to say no to the good things in life.

11th House · This brings luck in networking and wealth in an ever-expanding circle of friends and associates. You'll tend to hang out with philosophical groups and friends, as well as generous ones.

Jupiter in aspect to another planet

In aspect to another planet, Jupiter expands on how that planet functions. An easy aspect suggests good fortune while the challenging ones suggest you might be overdoing it and need to pull back.

Moon · Enhances emotional joy, trust and openness. You're excited about life on an emotional level and tend to have a lot of emotional connections.

Mars · You have an abundance of energy and perhaps do things to excess while somehow making just the right move at just the right time. Your actions are lucky.

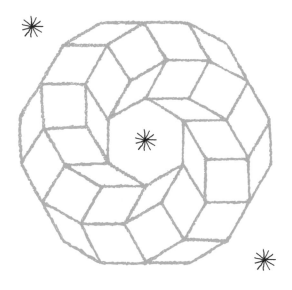

Saturn
Put a ring on it

Responsibility · Consolidation
Limitation · Discipline · Mastery · Time

RULES Capricorn
RULES 10th House
RULES skin, bones, teeth and knees
ASTROLOGICAL ORBITAL TIME: 29 years
TRANSITS EACH ZODIAC SIGN 2.5 years
STRONG in Libra, Capricorn and Aquarius
NEEDS CONSCIOUS EFFORT in Aries, Cancer and Leo

Sixth planet from the Sun and the last one visible to the naked eye, Saturn once represented the limits of space for most of human existence. For this reason it was symbolised as the Grim Reaper. It represents time and the finite: when time's up, it's up.

The sickle shape of its glyph refers to the harvest, as Saturn was named after the Roman god of agriculture. The glyph for Saturn also depicts the cross of matter over spirit. Earth realm comes first: do the work it takes to bring your ambition into material reality. Saturn's gift of boundaries helps crystallise our personality and sense of self. It describes what it is we become known for.

Saturn says: if you like it put a ring on it. The ringed planet of commitment, responsibility and long-term effort is here to batten down the hatches, pull the plug on excess and make sure we step up to the plate. Our dreams will only ever be a reality with actual hard work behind the manifesting.

There is no get-out-of-jail-free card with Saturn. Hard work and years of tunnelling your way to freedom with nothing but a plastic teaspoon is the only way you'll get where you need to go under Captain No Fun. Sounds like a total buzz-kill, right? If you like to suffer and work then you'll love it when Saturn lays its hand on you. If not, this is exactly what you need to stop fantasising, procrastinating or avoiding and start doing.

You'll feel like you're being punished, beaten into shape by an old-school blacksmith. In the end the effort is worth the outcome of creating just what you want and need. Saturn is associated with fate, therefore we're often unable to avoid what's on the cards for us, whether we like it or not.

When you work your Saturn, you agree to prioritise what's most important. Saturn is about the real deal, no fluff, no time wasting. The satisfaction of accomplishment, the reward of mastery and becoming an authority are its gifts.

Since it's associated with fear, adversity and obstacles, what goes up with Jupiter comes down with Saturn. It's the piano teacher who crushes your fingers into the keys when you clearly didn't do your practice, the headmistress who canes your knuckles when classes are skipped. It wants you to succeed in creating the life you want. It demands excellence, so its lessons can't be ignored. If you pay your dues on struggle street you're eventually rewarded by dint of your own effort. You'll reap the wisdom that only time and experience yields.

Overseeing boundaries and structure, Saturn rules our own outer casing (our physical limit in terms of the concept of the manifest self). The skeleton comes under Saturn's domain too, since it's hard and provides the ultimate structure for our otherwise soft bodies. The trick to Saturn is to balance rigidity with enough flexibility so as not to break, and to flow enough to not become dry and brittle.

Overdoing your Saturn

An overdone Saturn will be hardening, limiting, fearful and inflexible, impeding growth or risk taking. Boundaries will be too controlled, resulting in isolation, depression and disconnection. An unbalanced Saturn may lead to taking on too much of others' work or problems, feeling too responsible for others or struggling under the weight of the world. This is the workaholic type.

The antidote
Take time for self-care and nurturing, connection, fun and self-expression. Since Saturn is all about structure, give it a place in your life, then schedule in the fun and creativity. If you're

travelling, have 'free days' to wander and discover. Lessen the control over your experiences. Allow change and novelty with no expectation of the outcome. If you're shouldering too much burden, delegate. You're not responsible for everyone, but you are responsible for yourself. Say 'no' to being guilt-tripped.

Underdoing your Saturn

It can take sheer force of will to work your Saturn, and let's face it, it's not always the first priority when there are fun and good times to be had. Without the balance Saturn represents, you'll lack staying power. You won't put in the effort it takes to achieve something that takes time, like your life-purpose or dreams. You may give away your authority to others, losing control over your own life. Boundaries will be weak, so you may be drained or taken advantage of, or have a weakened sense of self. Ageing won't bring the benefits it should.

The antidote
Bring in Saturn by writing yourself a schedule, and set your alarm and reminders. Plan, strategise and prioritise what you want to achieve. If you really have no discipline, enroll in a course that will provide structure, learn by apprenticeship or find another organised system that will get you where you want to go. Working your way up in a larger company could be the path for you. And give back: once you have completed a certain level of mastery in a subject, mentor others. This can be a reciprocal cycle which establishes and builds your authority, self-respect and self-mastery. Check in with yourself, rather than seeking validation from others.

Saturn in your chart

Saturn in a sign
The sign Saturn is in indicates what you need to work long and hard at, what you're serious about and what you need to master over time. The sign can describe an aspect of career aptitude. It also reveals what you may find difficult or limited.
Virgo · You bring a serious attitude to personal conduct, manners

and efficiency. You may rewrite the rule book or pass on your thorough knowledge of etiquette. You'll learn streamlining and detail. Mastery of something intricate like classical guitar would be a fulfilling outlet: practice makes perfect!

Sagittarius · Takes study seriously and consolidates knowledge into a workable system. You may travel for work or even work in travel and education. You'll need to mould your ideals into something tangible you can live by. You may face fears around risk-taking and growth, sometimes ignoring opportunities and staying in the safe lane.

Saturn in a house

The house Saturn occupies in your birth chart is the area of life where you work at mastering an aspect of yourself or have boundaries, and also where you may feel limited or stuck. It's an area of life you may struggle with initially, yet through experience and sheer effort you can step into your authority.

2nd House · Regarding values and money, you work long and hard to build resources. You're the type of person who dutifully pays off the mortgage on a humble but centrally located apartment, eating at home instead of in fancy restaurants.

11th House · This placement suggests you will seek older friends who are serious, ambitious and career oriented. You feel responsible for your friends and perhaps lead groups or create your own.

Saturn in aspect to another planet

In aspect, Saturn tends to limit and focus the expression of any personal planet it's connected to.

Sun · This is the embodiment of self-reliant, dependable and hardworking grit. You shine brighter over time and have a natural maturity and reserve. You may find it hard to express who you are and this will be part of your life's work. You radiate authority and tend to take on responsibility.

Venus · This lends commitment in relationships, yet limits the overall number. You're not one to rush in and tend to be very reliable. You may prefer an older partner and to socialise with more mature friends.

Chiron
Wounded healer

Shamanism · Primal wound
Alienation · Holistic integration · Initiation

RULES Chiron doesn't have a sign rulership
RULES one's past hurt or deepest wound
ASTROLOGICAL ORBITAL TIME 51 years
TRANSITS EACH ZODIAC SIGN 2–9 years

Chiron is an asteroid, an outsider locked into an elliptical orbit that wanders between Saturn and Uranus.

Chiron represents primal, often accidental, wounding. It asks us to recognise and understand our wound and healing journey, and then recognise the condition in others, and help them heal. This process explains Chiron's alternative title, 'the wounded healer'.

In Greek mythology, Chiron was a centaur who voluntarily went into bondage to release Prometheus from eternal suffering, taking his place. By doing so Chiron was at last able to die, benefiting himself by becoming a god. Illustrated again is the idea of transcending to a higher place through service and connecting with a higher power, which releases us from our initial mode of suffering and torment.

When reading Chiron, remind yourself that we all have this mark of adversity in our chart and life somewhere. Focus on becoming consciously aware of it while balancing the obvious drawbacks with the hidden benefits. In what way has this wound deepened your experience and understanding of yourself and others? In what way can you help others through what you've learned? How can you bridge the gap between being a victim or outsider and becoming someone who can step up and help others with similar issues? Chiron is the rose garden in full bloom – the manure the bushes have grown through creates the glorious flowers.

Overdoing your Chiron

This occurs when you project your Chiron, your own wounding, attempting to fix everyone else as a distraction from dealing with your own pain.

The antidote
Healer, heal thyself first. Only then can you go to the next level and heal others. Create your own healing feedback loop.

Underdoing your Chiron

When you repress the wounded part of yourself, it becomes rejected and projected onto others so you revile, reject or exclude them. You're unable to perceive those issues within yourself. What triggers you in others are red flags and tell you what you need to reflect on.

By taking the role of 'healer' and seeing others as 'wounded' you cast them in a role where they live out your 'shadow' for you. You may be the one doing the wounding, passing on your troubles to someone else, then trying to leave your pain by leaving them.

The antidote
Mentor others, knowing triggers will come up for you – the key to healing is using your experience to assist others.

Chiron in your chart

Chiron in a sign
The sign Chiron is in indicates the nature of what your wounding is. The sign points to the nature of the wound, therefore the nature of the medicine.

Taurus · This indicates wounding around self-worth, beauty and money. 'Things' and 'stuff' take on a loaded meaning for you, or perhaps there's a loss that really cuts you, or there's an issue with quality. There is wounding around values – perhaps you have been rejected due to your unique views, leaving you feeling like an outsider.

Libra · This suggests sensitivity to equality in relationships. If you have this placement you may feel rejected as an equal and perhaps unfairly judged. Healing and a higher expression can come from practising radical fairness and justice. How can you help others that haven't been given a fair deal?

Chiron in a house

The house Chiron occupies in your birth chart is where you'll feel like an outsider, wanderer or exile from the status quo. It's where you won't fit in; it's where you'll feel left out, abandoned or rejected. There can be an experience or feeling of initiation and a hero's journey that will make you step up. Accepting your difference is part of healing your wounds.

5th House · The wounding may be associated with your ability to have fun with childlike abandon; perhaps you'll feel rejected by lovers and you'll need some help with creative expression.

8th House · Sex, death and other people's cash are sensitive issues. Perhaps you feel you missed out on an inheritance and still carry a chip on your shoulder, or have issues expressing your deeper, intimate side; you might feel rejected and experience pressure to conform. How can you help others who have been denied what is rightfully theirs? Or perhaps to reclaim parts of themselves they were taught to hide and reject by conforming?

Chiron in aspect to another planet

In aspect to another planet, Chiron brings the potential for sensitivity, understanding and healing. The planet aspected may be a part of you that's connected with the primal wound. Alternatively it could indicate how you heal others and the nature of your ability.

Sun · There may be wounds around self-expression, identity and building ego. A journey of self-healing and self-discovery is suggested. You'll understand how to support others in claiming their right to express themselves confidently and authentically.

Moon · There may be wounds around emotions, home, nurturing or perhaps rejection. Take yourself on an emotional healing journey and learn to nurture yourself. You'll know how to make others feel secure and safe.

Uranus
Shock of the new

Ingenuity · Sudden change · Originality
Reform · Revolution · Technology

RULES Aquarius
RULES 11th House
RULES electrical impulses of the nervous system
ASTROLOGICAL ORBITAL TIME 84 years
TRANSITS EACH ZODIAC SIGN 7 years
STRONG in Aquarius
NEEDS CONSCIOUS EFFORT in Leo

Seventh from the Sun, Uranus is the third largest planet in our solar system. With bragging rights to the coldest planetary atmosphere, it's as cool as a cucumber. Known as an ice giant, it has frozen water as part of its composition. Its look is calm, smooth and featureless. While most planets spin vertically, Uranus spins horizontally. Its poles are where its equator should be, and like the Mad Hatter, its upside down is the right way up. Where Uranus blows its winds of change, apply the motto 'expect the unexpected'.

Uranus rules the sign of Aquarius, sharing its futuristic, cutting-edge and progressive radicalism. It indicates unexpected change. Associated with the sky and hence the mind and ideas, it rules technological advancement, innovation and discovery.

Uranus cattle-prods us out of our comfort zone and into the whirl of life with the shock of the new. It is radical in its approach, genius in its vision and completely uncensored! Buckle up and get ready for the ride of your life. Resistance will only overload your circuits and cause change to manifest itself as crisis and cataclysm.

The role Uranus plays is one of irrevocable change. Systems will be challenged, traditions updated. This is an intellectual, a free-thinking and high-voltage archetype. It is set on cracking apart anything fixed or rigid. Its method is to shatter like a jackhammer on cement. Welcome in revelation, flashes of insight, sudden moments of clarity and a vision that cuts loose old paradigms.

Social change and ideals come under the influence of Uranus, and they are often tied closely with changing technology. You make the changes you need to and are keen to try new things. This planet is icy, and with too much Uranus, ideals for a larger humanitarian cause can lack heart and care for the individual. Uranus can be irresponsible and impulsive, resulting in chaotic upheaval. However, it gets the job done when needed and the calm after the storm may be worth it.

Uranus indicates where and how we create our own rules, march to the beat of our own drum and generally require freedom. Freedom of thought, freedom to try new things. If you are expressing your Uranus, you can work with groups yet retain your independence. You easily express your individuality and unique ideas, while detachment allows you to coolly listen to others' opinions and needs and remain aware of your own requirements and differences.

Overdoing your Uranus

Too much Uranus would mean constant instability, overreacting to stimuli and rebelling without a cause. You could find it hard to keep order and constancy in your life. Your nerves might be frazzled with energy, you could be out of touch with your body and feel out of step with the world around you.

Sudden endings could disrupt life and you could feel like a loner, isolated from others. Misunderstandings could become a theme. With the voltage turned up to high on Uranus, detachment can be overdone, ending with the mad-scientist type who lacks ethics, morals or compassion in their pursuit of an outcome. Too much intellectualising and you'll become ungrounded. When you're lost in a world of ideas, losing touch with the body and daily reality, it's a short step to depression, confusion, isolation and, in extreme times, madness.

The antidote

Drop into your body by acknowledging your physical sensations, breath, taste, touch, smell. Ground yourself in nature. Detoxify from the digital world, and even put down the book. Listen to others and notice the responses your body has to them. Notice the vibes you pick up around you when there's silence.

Underdoing your Uranus

Underdoing or projecting Uranus traits by not making the changes you need in your life will instead cause the changes to be thrust upon you. For example, if you need a career change and haven't made the leap, you may find you are suddenly fired or made redundant. If you need relationship change, your partner may do the leaving for you.

Projecting parts of yourself that you don't accept because they're too different, unusual or radical may leave you feeling triggered when you see others living them out with seeming gay abandon. This is the red flag: it's possibly your problem, not theirs, and deserves some reflection.

The antidote

Own your quirks and your genius. Embody the change you want to see in the world. Support the visionary part of yourself that demands an independent position in order to see clearly. Create and take the space you need. Nervous tension needs to be channelled and grounded. Ask yourself where you need to make a change in your life, where you need freedom and what part of yourself needs expression.

Uranus in your birth chart

Uranus in a sign

The sign Uranus is in indicates what flavour of change and genius you require.

Capricorn · You'll be a game-changing entrepreneur seeking freedom in business, or hoping to start new, unusual businesses.

Aquarius · You'll be drawn to unusual group endeavours and you might employ tech to bring together like-minded groups. Equality and fraternity are important.

Uranus in a house

The house Uranus occupies in your birth chart is where you need stimulation and change. You bring a new way of thinking to this area and require freedom at all costs.

2nd House · There could be sudden changes in fortune. You'll be a financial risk taker, and you'll borrow or lend money. There could be unusual ways of making cash – some shocking or non-traditional. All this means you could be unreliable with money or a genius at making it. You could have humanitarian or unusual values that routinely undergo change.

4th House · Your parents may have been unusual or radical. Your home may be unusual or you might have an unconventional living arrangement.

Uranus in aspect to another planet

In aspect to another planet, Uranus brings energy, as well as changeable behaviour, to how that planet functions.

Mercury · This can lend a radical perspective as well as cutting-edge ideas. Communication style can be unusual, unique or gifted. There could be bursts of communication and ideas.

Mars · There can be genius new ways of doing things, as well as some erratic behaviour. Energy levels are high and motivation can come in spurts.

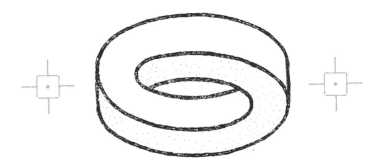

Neptune
Let there be unicorns

**Oneness · Dissolution · Divinity
Surrender · Mysticism · Sensitivity · Imagination**

RULES Pisces
RULES 12th House
RULES pineal gland
ASTROLOGICAL ORBITAL TIME 165 years
TRANSITS EACH ZODIAC SIGN 13.75 years
STRONG in Pisces
NEEDS CONSCIOUS EFFORT in Virgo

An ice giant, Neptune is eighth from the Sun and the last official planet in our astrological line-up. This vivid blue sphere's high pressure causes it to literally rain diamonds.

Named after the Roman god of the sea, its glyph is shaped like a trident. That can also be viewed as a tuning fork with its prongs pointing upward, ready to pick up all the vibes. Neptune has a soft and compassionate touch, plus empathy, love of animals and attraction to art and the mystical.

Neptune is all about taking things onwards and upwards. Its purpose is to dissolve, soften and make permeable in order to merge everything into oneness. Merging means boundaries have to go. Death of the ego or sense of self is the way to harness Neptune. Spiritual leaders, gurus and great artists have learned to straddle mundane reality and the divine space within.

We all harbour a deep, undefined longing for transcendence of our 'self' into that greater formless union with oneness. Neptune in our chart represents how and where we are likely to experience, find or search for that spiritual or mystical union: the awareness of being borderless, limitless and at one with all. That sense of being beyond time and place.

The ultimate blossoming of Neptune is attaining a state of nirvana, but being able to toggle between it and a solid ability to function in everyday reality. We want to be able to go

Planets

beyond identifying with the limited collection of ideas that form our sense of self or ego, but wear it lightly: that's the goal of most spiritual traditions.

All the religious traditions at their core speak in terms of Neptune's realm. Prayer, meditation, mantra, fasting, trance, music or other art forms that transport you beyond yourself and this moment in time and space are all ways of entering Neptune's realm. The true gateway to spiritual bliss is highly personal, internal and completely immaterial.

The way to Neptune's promised land is fraught with halls of smoke and mirrors, confusion, deception and illusion. Like the sign of Pisces that Neptune rules, this element of our life or self is a slippery fish. The more we try to grasp or define Neptune, the more it eludes us – like grasping at a mirage. Completely the opposite of Saturn's crystallising material realm, it is not of this world. Actively making our way to the Neptunian part of ourselves is a passive pursuit of surrender. It can't be coerced or forced. Sometimes the best way is to bend and give in to it through meditation or selfless acts of compassion, love and charity.

Seen as a higher octave of Venus, the planet of personal love, Neptune's gateway consists of an impersonal love of all beings. The heart chakra needs to be unchecked and open without judgment while the crown chakra located in the pineal gland is a path to higher vibrations and visions. Meditation on these two centres can be revealing – give it a try as you reach out with love to all, near and far. Be open and non-judgemental, and notice both what you feel and what you see.

Overdoing your Neptune

Too much Neptune may result in you becoming a psychic sponge, soaking up impressions and losing the shore of your sense of self. Extreme sensitivity can result in allergies, illness, toxicity or a general malaise.

Traction is lost in the material world of having to turn up on time, work and pay bills. Say goodbye to responsibility and hello to flaky. Drifting is a problem with Neptune, as is escapism, resulting in dependency on others or a substance.

The day-to-day grind can be overwhelming, as heightened ideals don't match the gritty everyday reality.

You'll be open season for deception, or perhaps you're the one casting a deceitful spell over others. You may become lost in illusion, fantasy or self-deception. In the extreme, your grip on reality can completely unravel.

The antidote

Muscle in some Saturnian definition, boundaries, self-control and discipline. Get a watch and wear it, set reminders or invest in a virtual assistant to keep you on track and take care of details such as, oh, paying the rent. It's OK to have personal boundaries and say 'no'. Join a class, group or course that can act as a container for you to plug into the creative or spiritual realms without becoming lost. When you're souped up on Neptune in this life, it can be worthwhile working in a field where Neptune is a superpower rather than a hindrance. Art teacher, yoga instructor, writer, healer...

Underdoing your Neptune

In modern society, spiritual poverty. As with so much in life, the answer is within and the only way to find it is to consult our own inner oracle. If you're applying an external fix to fill an inner void, you're most likely on the wrong path.

You may not want to own or take responsibility of the less glamorous side of Neptune, instead you may cast others in a role to play out your 'unacceptable' parts, taking the onus off you. However, dealing with Neptune externally won't work.

The antidote

The traits you see as unacceptable or that trigger you deserve a closer look. Reflect on where you may be repressing those traits in yourself. Always attracted to chaotic, creative types? Consider what kind of message you have internalised from your past. If you can dig this out and reclaim your right to express yourself in Neptunian ways, you're more likely to stop attracting chaos. These moments are an opportunity and a mirror.

Neptune in your chart

Neptune in a sign
The sign Neptune is in describes what your mystic style is and how you relate to the divine within yourself.

Neptune is currently in Pisces from 2012 until 2025 and we're feeling the effects. We've already seen a rise in interest in transcendent techniques and language: think of mindfulness and yoga going mainstream. Vegan and vegetarian lifestyles are being adopted en-masse (reflecting Neptunian compassion), and words like 'cosmic' and 'mystic' are more likely to invite intrigue than the eyerolls they did only a few years ago.

Neptune in a house
The house Neptune is in indicates the area of life where you experience bliss or confusion and illusion.

3rd House · This results in an ability to experience the divine in everyday moments. You don't need to venture off to the Himalayas to find redemption. You'll see the divine in your latte.

8th House · This placement indicates that you tap into the divine when you merge with others, either intimately or via a business. Watch for deception, as this is also an area of vulnerability, thanks to Neptune's lack of boundaries or eye for solid detail.

Neptune in aspect to another planet
In aspect to another planet, Neptune tends to dissolve and diffuse its expression while heightening sensitivity.

Moon · Turns up the dial emotionally on compassion, sensitivity and empathy. Your gut instincts are particularly sensitive, so trust them. You are kind and impressionable emotionally.

Mars · Artistic or spiritual pursuits will help energise you. Not all those who wander are lost, but with this placement sometimes they actually are! Practise acting on a hunch or your intuition: you'll surprise yourself.

Pluto
Alchemy

**Something hidden · Transformation · Regeneration
Deep insight · Intensity · Power · Elimination**

RULES Scorpio
RULES 8th House
RULES processes of elimination and expulsion
ASTROLOGICAL ORBITAL TIME 240 years
TRANSITS EACH ZODIAC SIGN 11–30 years
STRONG in Aries and Scorpio
NEEDS CONSCIOUS EFFORT in Taurus and Libra

Great things come in small packages. On the edge of the solar system, Pluto is the smallest planet. Ninth from the Sun, Pluto tolerated its official demotion from planet to dwarf planet in 2006. Coincidentally, we all like to bury or ignore things that Pluto represents rather than face them head-on. While astronomers may want to minimise Pluto, in astrology it retains its meaning. As we now know, what's ignored psychologically tends to control us until we face and deal with it.

Named after the Roman god of the underworld, Pluto is a deep, penetrating and compulsive force bent on renewal at any cost. The change we experience through Pluto is thorough and complete, and resistance is useless. What needs to be purged will be, regardless of consequence. It is the ultimate survivalist, one that will employ any level of violence, force or ruthlessness to achieve its ambition.

Pluto brings our darkest behaviours to the ground so it can resurrect us authentically. Its treasure is always hidden – it requires alchemy to turn darkness into gold. Think of the caterpillar in the chrysalis stage – it must seem akin to annihilation. However, we know it has to die to some degree to be reborn. The chrysalis is the place we find ourselves in when we are in the throes of a Plutonic metamorphosis. Allowing the process to run its course, rather than halting it with chemicals or repression, results in rebirth. When we're completely new, light and free of the caterpillar stage, we know it was worth the journey.

Pluto is intense: there's no prettying it up. It can be dark, painful and downright horrifying to face our most reviled yet often most powerful aspects. However, when you work with its energy or situation truthfully and willingly, it represents the most liberating action of all the planets.

Representing where we have limitless personal resources and power, Pluto is a bit like our inner atom bomb. It can remain in the depths of unconsciousness and implode, annihilating us, or we can use its immense energy to completely transform and empower ourselves. The energy of Pluto is extremely difficult to manage, let alone control. It's hard to command our inner reserves of power and potential. However, the change will happen whether we choose it or it's thrust upon us, so it's best to conduct it consciously.

The movement of Pluto through the signs is so slow it leaves its signature on an entire generation. Like a dark goddess on a mission, it has 11 to 30 years in one sign alone to affect extreme change. It's thorough and will be remembered for the sometimes violent, destructive approach to alteration. The sign it's in reveals the area that a particular generation will be laser-focused on destroying and hell-bent on transforming, as well as the areas that will be purged.

Overdoing your Pluto

The ultimate power tripper, you use your great force and magnetism to control and manipulate others. If power struggles are a regular feature of your life, it's not them, it's you. In the grip of a lust haze, are you obsessed? Finding it hard to let go of a lover or project, the desire burning you up? A compulsive need to transform both yourself and your environment leaves you unable to maintain consistency in life or relationships.

The antidote
Let go of control, bring in trust. Psychology as well as psychotherapy is the domain of Pluto. Search your depths to

find the gold hidden in the darkness. If you're overdoing your Pluto due to loss of power or abuse in the past, it's time to get guidance, face up to it and regain your power and trust in the Universe. Your ability to completely transform your life lies buried under the demons that haunt you. Choose you.

Underdoing your Pluto

You give away your power to others, finding yourself dominated and controlled. Betrayal is a repeating theme. Attracting jealous, obsessive or possessive lovers and friends seems to be a feature of your life, and you're afraid to step up and take control or change your situation or behaviour patterns.

You know you desperately need to change some toxic areas of your life, yet you're fearful of the death and rebirth you know it will take to transform it into what you truly desire.

The antidote
Time to reclaim your power. Draw in assistance if you have to and be prepared to let areas of your life and behaviour patterns completely die in order to renew yourself.

Pluto in your chart

Pluto in a sign
The sign Pluto is in indicates what you are compelled to transform. It also reveals the flavour of your reinvention.

Currently Pluto is in Capricorn (2008–2024), which rules large companies, business, authority and responsibility. Its current agenda? Dismantling outdated government and big business structures, while companies wrestle for power over people, resources and patents. Pluto made its grand entrance to Capricorn in 2008 with its usual destructive force in the biggest global financial meltdown since the Great Depression, and in the meantime the #metoo movement is gaining unstoppable traction. This is a classic example of Pluto's function of elimination: to draw out what has been festering and hidden in order to detox and renew.

Pluto in a house

The house Pluto occupies in your birth chart is the area of your life where you will encounter the need to own your power and reinvent until you do. Old behaviour patterns will become ripe for destruction and renewal. You may meet intense, transformative Plutonian types in this area of life and you will emit a personal magnetism. You will have and seek deep insight here.

5th House · Your creations are powerful. You have deep reserves of creative energy. Romance is no light matter for you and will be transformative. You'll seek intensity and deep connection right off the bat and play for keeps (try not to get obsessed!). Breezy fun and self expression are rarely on the menu – exploring mysteries is your idea of a good time.

7th House · You attract intense partners and desire transformation within relationships. You do well with a partner who is keen to engage in personal growth consciously. When facing your darkest aspects through your close relationships, obsession could be a feature, as well as the difficult feelings of betrayal and control issues.

Pluto in aspect to another planet

In aspect to another planet, Pluto contributes intensity and power to how that planet functions. The function of the planet in aspect will undergo transformation throughout your life and become a source of magnetic personal power.

Sun · You're a powerful personality, magnetic and charismatic – you won't be ignored. You have energy to burn, and then some. Watch for dominating tendencies: if others are controlling you it means you need to step up into your personal power. You'll be compelled to reinvent yourself throughout your life.

Venus · The original love bomber. It's all about the power of love, or the love of power! Depending on how easy or challenging Pluto's relationship is to your Venus, this is a line you may have to walk. Love and money are loaded and involve power issues. You will transform through relationships and love. You need depth and loyalty in all of your relationships.

Nodes
Destiny calling

A particularly interesting component of astrology for the modern mystic are the nodes. These are destiny points in your birth chart (based on the Moon's orbit around Earth), and are represented by the two symbols above – the one on the left is north, the one on the right is south. It's useful to identify where these fall in your chart and what they represent. They are always directly opposite each other, so if only your north node is indicated, draw a direct line through the chart to position your south node.

South node

This points to your past – some say it is your past lifetimes and the gifts these past lives have bought into your current life. In general, the position (sign and house) of the south node indicates your comfort zone, where your strengths lie and where you feel most at home. You might feel comfortable there, but it's important to stretch yourself and push out of this zone, otherwise you could become stagnated and stuck. The goal is to aim for your true north, your destiny.

North node

This area of life (as indicated by the node's placement in sign and house) is underdeveloped, therefore unfamiliar. When you work towards developing it, you'll find things tend to work out and the best of you will begin to shine. Occasionally we can take a big black limo downtown to our south node for a bit of comfort and indulgence, but chip away in the direction of your true north to let the Universe know you're doing what you can to help it help you!

Nodes in a sign

North node in Virgo (south node in Pisces) · Your comfort zone is Piscean. You are in touch with how the Universe works and are sensitive to the subtle, even psychic realms. However, staying in your comfort zone means being disorganised and escaping responsibilities. Aim north to Virgo (detail) and tackle the mundane, menial tasks, maintain a routine and take care of responsibilities – you'll find this brings out the best in you.

North node in Aquarius (south node in Leo) · Your comfort zone is being a VIP (Leo). Your self confidence is palpable, you're creative and easily in touch with your inner child. You know you're in your comfort zone when you think it's all about you. Redirect toward your Aquarius north node by applying detachment. Consider the bigger picture as well as others. How can you use your confidence and creativity for the greater good of the group?

Nodes in a house

North node 10th House (south node 4th House) · Your comfort zone is in the family nest (4th House) and you cleave to home. This lifetime calls you to stand on that firm base that comes so easily, but then to push out into the world. Face the unknown by leaving your family duty or concerns behind so you can develop your career potential or contribute to the community (10th House of career and public image). Get your personal brand up and out there and face the fear of curating your public image.

North node 7th House (south node 1st House) · This placement suggests you're very comfortable with your sense of self (1st House of personality). You can strike out and do your own thing. In your previous life it was all about you. However, relationships and teaming up one-on-one are foreign. Partnership (as represented by the 7th House) is the direction you need to head toward. Learn to compromise, work together and take others' needs into consideration to create win-win scenarios in which you'll grow. Bring your strong sense of self to a partnership so you don't get lost.

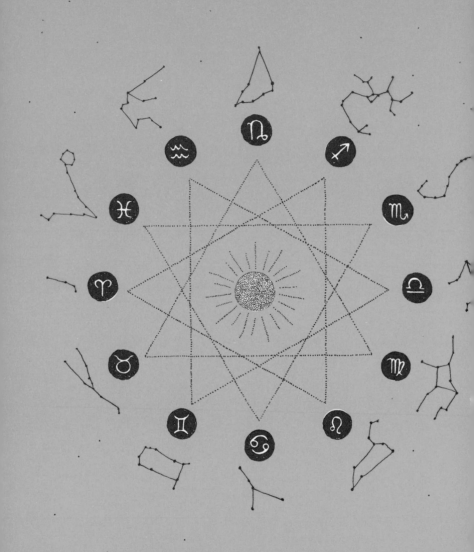

II. Signs

What's your star sign? Your answer could be the only bit of astro knowledge you have – which is a good start, because it's such a key part of your birth chart! Your sign (also known as a Sun sign) is determined by which of the 12 signs the Sun was in during the month you were born. The Sun's function – a sense of self, self-expression and identity – is expressed in this sign, so the placement of this planet is very revealing.

But your Sun sign isn't the only planet/sign combo you should be aware of. On the day you were born, all the planets will have been positioned within certain signs. As you might remember, the planets represent 'what' is being expressed, the sign it is in shows 'how' this function is expressed. So to get your inner mystic rolling, read this chapter to understand the characteristics of each sign, then identify which signs the planets are positioned in within your birth chart. Each planetary position (through the filter of a sign) will reveal a particular aspect of your nature.

If you get lost, or the meaning of the signs is blurring or blending, go back to keywords and simplify. For example, if Venus (love) is in the sign of Aries (assertive), you will likely express your love directly and assertively. And what will you be attracted to? Forthrightness and trailblazers! It's as simple as that.

Aries
I am

**Independent · Assertive · Active
Impulsive · Pioneering · Enthusiastic
Fearless**

MARCH 21 – APRIL 19
RULER Mars
ELEMENT Fire
MODE Cardinal
HOUSE Associated with the 1st House
RULES The head
PERSONALITY Extroverted
COLOUR Red

Just do it! While everyone else is talking, crying or counting their Insta-likes, Aries has already finished and signed off for the day. Quick on action and low on patience, Mars-ruled Aries needs to feel the rush of excitement that comes from tackling new challenges head-on.

The opposite of what's traditionally considered a 'good girl', she's bold, loud and here to fight the fight. 'I am a delicate feminine flower,' said no Aries ever. She develops and learns about herself by wrestling with problems. Eating risk for breakfast, Aries hates to be bored and doesn't do waiting. Try to keep up!

Entrepreneurial and adversarial by nature, Aries types are perfectly positioned to blaze trails, from high octane start-ups to careers involving rapid-fire decision making. Needless to say she likes to be in charge, she's a born leader and she won't back down from opposition. In fact, watch her thrive on the challenge of beating you and aceing her personal best.

Physically this sign rules the head, often lending Aries a thick, straight brow, aquiline nose and statement 'get out of my way' stare. She leans into life. Look for those tell-tale scars, as accidents and even bumps to the head can be par for the course. Headaches mean too much steam has built up, and firestorm outbursts are definitely a thing. The original adrenaline junkie, Aries needs physical outlets like athletics or yoga – but even getting in the car and going for a drive can be therapeutic.

A Fire sign, Aries loves her flames to be scorching, like the burst of a furnace door opening. Being Cardinal Fire, she emits an almighty blast of energy, but as she's quickly bored she's soon on to the next big challenge.

If you are an Aries, you know by now that your greatest strength is in your spirited courage to forge into uncharted territory and stand your ground. If those around you are looking at you in sheer terror, you know you're headed in the right direction. They'll catch up next century!

Classic Aries
Lady Gaga

Bursting onto the global stage like a modern-day Amazon, Lady Gaga has both Sun and Venus in this warrior sign. She uses her music and videos as a vehicle to make statements and fearlessly take risks, and she voices strong opinions on the issues most important to her.

Aries is often called the baby of the zodiac. Drawing on her wellspring of life force, Aries confidently greets the world stating: 'I am what I am.' Gaga's track 'Born This Way' cemented her as an icon and leader in self-acceptance.

Gaga demonstrates how being a strong woman and stepping outside socially sanctioned behaviour (and dress) pays off. The more she spoke out on issues closest to her heart, the more fans felt heard and represented.

Ready to rumble? Classic Aries traits in Gaga are that hard look of determination, strong voice, bold lyrics and brave courting of controversy. Aries types are brazen and big on throwing it all in the ring. Daring in everything she does, Lady Gaga's costuming, and sometimes lack of it, lays it all out on the line while simultaneously demanding acceptance. In her we see the image of the Ram, head down, charging full throttle, come what may.

Surviving the pitfalls of being an Aries

Innocence
You're sincere to a fault, straight-shooting and so upfront you expect others to be the same. Hidden agendas trip you up. You overcome setbacks quickly; however, it helps to gain insight from those who understand the complexities of other people. And learn to use your quick intuition to dodge those keen to draw you into tangled webs and sticky situations.

Keep true to your course
Don't drop your speed to make others feel comfortable. By now you know you're born to lead – surge forth and stand up for what you know is right. Play to your strengths and find an area where you can propel yourself towards achievement and personal frontiers.

Consider the polarity of Libra
Remember it takes two to tango. Aries is such an independent, solo sign. You can be accused of being tactless, insensitive and self-centred. On one hand, you could take note from the polarity of Libra, which is about understanding points of view other than your own. On the other hand, we could all learn from you about how to operate from a centred place of self. Sometimes others take offence simply because they aren't asserting themselves in the world as you are.

Find your fire starter
The right bae for you loves your Spitfire speed, courage and gumption. You could find a softer person helps to bring out your sensitive side and connect with your vulnerability. They will appreciate that you can take control and bring excitement into their life. Do they enjoy adventure? Can they keep up with you? A common cause you can both get behind can be an exciting aphrodisiac. If they are able to give you the space you need, you may have a keeper. You like to let it all hang out, so your intended needs to accept and love you as much as you accept and love yourself.

Cosying up to an Aries

Increase the adrenaline

Take them to new hot spots, get them moving, keep the pace snappy. Physical adventures like whitewater rafting or skydiving ought to do the trick. They love intellectual challenges, so spice up your convo with new ideas and concepts, and be prepared for some friendly, possibly heated, debate. They're not angry, they're passionate!

Be direct

Beat around the bush and Aries will miss your signals. Say it like you mean it – with passion and enthusiasm.

Challenge them

Aries' Achilles heel is their inability to refuse a challenge. Fire them up by throwing down the gauntlet. If you can beat them at their own game they'll respect you for it and see your worth. Aries love conquest, remember, so let them chase you.

Aries in your chart
You might not be an Aries, but you'll still feel the Aries vibe

Look at your birth chart, and locate the area ruled by Aries. In this area you'll be active and assertive, and seek challenge.

House · With Aries on the cusp of the 8th House of shared resources, sex and death, you'll leap in where angels fear to tread.

On the cusp of the 11th House of social groups, you might be involved with organisations that look for the edge in anything from sports to business. You'll find your friends tend to be active and your attitude to social responsibility is forthright. You may find yourself leading groups of like-minded people.

Planet · Planets in Aries express their function directly and often impulsively. Venus (love) in Aries is alpha: you'll let others know if you like them and enjoy meeting new people.

Mars (action) in Aries is in the home sign, so standing up for yourself is easy. You'll have energy to burn and might need a high-impact exercise routine.

Taurus
I have

**Sensual · Resourceful · Fecund
Consistent · Enduring · Cautious
Determined**

APRIL 20 – MAY 20
RULER Venus
ELEMENT Earth
MODE Fixed
HOUSE Associated with the 2nd House
RULES The throat, neck and chest
PERSONALITY Introverted
COLOUR Autumnal golds, browns, greens

The first of the material girls, Earth sign Taurus is ready to make the most of what the world has to offer.

She's inestimably sensual: think honey dripping down the skin glacier-slow, lush velvet and ambient lighting.

Ruling planet Venus is grounded in this sign of fecund creativity. She asks, is it beautiful, practical, useful? She appreciates texture, natural materials and great design. All Earth signs work for and appreciate what money can buy, and Taurus is no exception. She'll toil hard and long for what she buys so she wants it to last. She may have expensive taste, but her resourceful nature means she will often find exactly what she wants at the best price. Taurus loves nothing more than a bargain. Oh, and pastries. Michelin-starred, ideally; cornershop at a pinch.

She acquires, accumulates and builds things that endure. Taureans cleave to all things solid and beautiful. The current 'built to break' ethos must have them shaking their head, rolling their eyes and heading for the nearest bespoke craftsperson.

Taurus likes her loves and friendships the same as she likes her money in the bank… to last and grow. She'll acquire you and feel she owns you for life. Nothing says BFF like the affectionate, solid consistency Taurus brings to the table.

When giving practical help, her famous patience can be tried on those that don't take steps to get themselves out of a mire. Less talk, more action. Taureans like to get on with it without fuss or complaint.

Since before it was trending, eco-living appealed to Taurus. She'll upcycle or repair before she casts anything out. Wastefulness is not her style.

This Earth sign tends to be the most comfortable and in touch with her body. Her body is her compass; she understands it knows everything. Instinctively cautious, Taurus has her own pace, which tends toward the rhythm of nature. From forest to sea, she craves contact with the natural world. This modern mystic senses the spirit of the land, the energy in the rocks and the breath in the trees.

She's methodical and won't be poked or prodded to perform at someone else's whim. If she's feeling harried or has a vague sense of 'not quite right', she'll apply the brakes and slow down even more. Stubborn, yes. A beast of burden, no.

Classic Taurus
Adele

Since Taurus rules the throat, it's not surprising that many well-known singers are ruled by this melodic sign. While the body part ruled by each sign can be a focal point, it can also be the first place to suffer due to imbalance. Taureans often endure throat issues or stiff necks and shoulders.

Taurus is a sign of acquisition as well as that of a gourmand, which often results in a robust and full physique. Movements are regular and calm, temperament is even.

Like all Taureans in tune with what matters most to them, Adele, at the height of fame, decided she needed a work/life balance and took several years off from her career. At one point she even took back her old job in a small record store. She also realised not many fans would relate to her life as a successful global star, so the move helped ground her lyrics in a more down-to-earth experience they could identify with.

Surviving the pitfalls of being a Taurus

Does your comfort zone fit
Old habits die hard. You don't like change, so you rarely leave your comfort zone. You have your own pace, but your opposite sign is Scorpio, whose impulse is to ruthlessly raze anything past its best in order to drive change. It takes this kind of no-holds-barred insistence to steer you into greener pastures when you cling to what you've outgrown. Draw on this polarity to balance any stubborn adherence to the familiar if it's no longer serving you. Know when it's time to consolidate and move forward.

Because you know you're worth it
Being an Earth sign, you value your material possessions and can confuse what you own with what you're worth. Reflect your inner worth into the outer world, not the other way around. Show off that internal abundance with concrete plans and focused practical action.

Find your forever bae
Your stability tends to attract those who are more out to sea emotionally and in life. Loyalty and the ability to bed-in for the long haul are essential, so make sure any potential partners are worth the investment, as you don't give away your heart easily. As a fixed sign it takes even longer to let go. Plus, any match will need to pile on the cuddles. Restaurateurs, gourmands and grounded hedonists may also apply.

Cosying up to a Taurus

Taste, touch, feel, see, listen...
Taurus is super-sensual, so appeal to their senses and pile on the affection. Meet-ups over food are ideal. Music holds special appeal, so share playlists or invite them to see live bands.

Nature's temple
Taurus is up for anything that involves communing with nature. Take them to their special place with a picnic, go on a hike or even go camping... hang on, make that glamping.

Get Taurus on your team

While Taureans know how to kick back and enjoy life's prizes, they also love to get things done. They make an excellent business or work colleague. If you have the start-up initiative, they have the stamina and resourcefulness to push projects through to fulfilment.

Taurus in your chart
You might not be a Taurus, but you'll still feel the Taurus vibe

Look at your birth chart and locate the area ruled by Taurus. In this area, you'll be practical and interested in both pleasure and material acquisition.

House · If Taurus rules your 7th House of equal partnership, you'll seek stability in your one-on-ones. They'll need to provide you with both material comforts and serenity. You're in for the long game, so take it step-by-step.

If your 9th House of personal philosophy, higher education and travel has a Taurus bias, you'll roam for practical reasons. You'll need to touch the architecture, bathe in the ambiance and enjoy local music and arts. You'll have set beliefs that will take a lot to change, if ever, or may evolve very slowly over your lifespan.

Planets · Planets expressing their function through the filter of Taurus will seek to ground themselves in practical application. Mars in Taurus seeks to act pragmatically and practically. You'll be robust, and loaded with plenty of endurance and stamina to reach your goals. Although it may take you longer to get there, you tend to finish in front in the end due to sheer persistence and focused effort.

When in Taurus, Mercury, ruler of mind and communications, is thoughtful and structured. You'll take your time with decisions and tend not to change your mind once it's made up. You're interested in how things work and in practical solutions rather than flaky concepts or emotional tangents. You may take longer to learn but this fixed sign has an infallible and long memory.

Gemini
I think

**Communicative · Curious · Clever
Dual-natured · Restless · Changeable
Trickster**

MAY 21 – JUNE 20
RULER Mercury
ELEMENT Air
MODE Mutable
HOUSE Associated with the 3rd House
RULES The shoulders, arms, hands, lungs
and nervous system
PERSONALITY Extroverted
COLOUR Silver

This sparkalicious sign is all about Air: intellect, speech, communication, connections. Ruled by quicksilver Mercury, Gemini is the most restless and curious cat on the street.

Everything with Gemini happens in double time. Nervous energy propels her forward to constantly discover new ideas then spread them like glitter blown from her palm.

She's the one you can take anywhere. Like her ruler Mercury, she has the ability and interest to cover all terrain. High, low, in, out: 'If you never ever go you'll never ever know,' she says. In myth, Gemini's ruler Mercury was depicted as having either a winged helmet, representing a speedy and flighty mind, or winged ankles, indicating an ability to move swiftly – with an access-all-areas pass.

Gemini is not a deep researcher. Intellectually she travels fast and light. She's busy, super-social and loves instant access to info. Twitter was made for her.

All the Air signs have a certain quality of coolness about them. The objectivity of the Air signs can be seen in Gemini through her impulse to look at everything as if through a prism. She wants all sides and all points of view. The 'gem' in Gemini is diamond: one of her symbols, and also known for its multifaceted clarity. Being Mutable, the Air element accentuates intellectual adaptability and responsiveness to external stimuli.

Born with the gift of the gab, she's known for her quick wit and repartee. Gemini talks – a lot. I've seen Gemini children chat to inanimate objects once their audience has tuned out.

Her mind has a high metabolic rate, frequently needing to be fed fresh ideas. She's super-bright and picks up trends and skills quickly. But just as today's hottest new fashion soon becomes so yesterday, she'll be onto the next one before you've even realised it was a thing. Geminis tend to stay quite youthful and hip since they don't stick to a style or outlook for long. They're quite happy to move with the times.

Another symbol helpful in understanding Gemini's unique gifts is the Chinese Tao concept of yin and yang. It says that nothing is either black or white. There is duality in everything. Yang is the external, the cut and thrust, the peak of the wave, or the hard teapot. Yin is the internal, soft and receptive, the trough of the wave or the tea in the pot. They're interdependent rather than existing in opposition. Gemini's symbol of twins represents this inherent duality. Those born under this sign have a love of puzzles in general, in particular paradoxes, as it takes their mind into that liminal twilight zone away from black-and-white thinking.

Gemini rules the nervous system which operates through contrast, as well as being the messenger service between brain and body. Whatever the form of communication, be it postal service, email, virtual chat or real chat, Gemini rules it all.

Physically Gemini has rulership over the shoulders, arms and hands, lending dexterity to anyone with strong placements in this sign. Notably, shoulders are well proportioned.

Classic Geminis
Azealia Banks and Iggy Azalea

Geminis' primary function of connecting and communicating has enabled both Azealia Banks and Iggy Azalea to carve out their own territory in the world of rap and hip hop. These two artists are unrelated and come from different backgrounds and countries, but both were born a year apart with the Sun in Gemini and they share qualities in terms of rapid-fire, crisp lyrics that speak from personal experience and reflect our times. When Gemini moves into roles that open up new lines of communication we see ourselves in reflection. We begin to know ourselves that bit more and move forward on our journey of self discovery. In this aspect Gemini is the modern mystic who writes and shares our story.

Classic Gemini II
Marilyn Monroe

Gemini's talent for acting derives from that Mutable versatility and ability to express multiple points of view. They can change roles or sides exceptionally quickly, giving rise to apparent moodiness and notorious propensity to be 'two faced'. Marilyn Monroe was able to respond to the market by playing upon a perception that beautiful women aren't intelligent. However, she was intelligent and she fought the studios throughout her career to gain more diverse and challenging roles.

Surviving the pitfalls of being a Gemini

Chilling
Your key to health is balance. Imbalance results in becoming flighty, scattered, frazzled and flaky. Although you'll resist slowing down, remember to take time to curl up quietly with a good book.

Get to the point
Too much chasing the next best thing can lead to a meaningless monologue of random facts and information. Balance it by drawing on the polarity of Sagittarius, which is all about connecting diverse information into a unified philosophy. Think: 'What is the point,' then find the meaning.

Find your twin flame
Gemini, you need a lot of airtime, so your perfect partner will need to have a love of listening. You'll thrive with someone who can keep up with you and stimulate your mind, while also encouraging you to recharge those overused batteries regularly. You love fun and games, so a partner that can be a light and upbeat playmate is better than a slower, deeper soul

who perhaps dwells on emotions. You like to change scene regularly, gallery-hop, bar-hop, even work-hop. Three social functions in a night? Yes please. Once again, your flame needs to either keep up or happily keep the home fires burning for when you finally come home.

Cosying up to a Gemini

Social butterfly

Geminis are social butterflies, so take them to meet-ups, do a short course together and accompany them to talks on anything they don't yet know about. Everything is interesting to Gemini... until the next thing comes along. This is how they introduce others to new ideas and why Gemini symbolises the messenger of the zodiac.

Gemini in your chart
You might not be a Gemini, but you'll still feel the Gemini vibe

Look at your birth chart and locate the area ruled by Gemini. In this area, you'll express duality, be ideas-focused and rely on your communication skills.

House · Gemini ruling the cusp of the 2nd House of resources most likely has more than one stream of income. You may make a living out of your quick mind and have no shortage of ideas on how to make money.

If Gemini rules the cusp of your 7th House of personal relationships, you'll need lots of chat time in your one-on-ones. You may even maintain two lovers!

Planet · If your Moon is in Gemini, you'll need to talk with a sense of immediacy about your emotions to feel connection and security. You absolutely can't be shut out or shut down.

If you have Mars in Gemini, you'll need to act on impulse and fare better with short-term projects, as your energy can't sustain gruelling long hauls.

Cancer
I feel

Caring · Nurturing · Protective
Shrewd · Sentimental · Empathetic
Family-oriented

JUNE 21 – JULY 22
RULER Moon
ELEMENT Water
MODE Cardinal
HOUSE Associated with the 4th House
RULES The breasts and stomach
PERSONALITY Introverted
COLOUR Opalescent white, jade/sea green

A Moonchild afloat in tides of fluctuating emotion, Cancer is the first of the Water signs and ruled by the Moon, rather than a planet proper.

Family is everything to Cancer. The Mother archetype is expressed through her – but note it's not the bored-housewife-on-valium version, but the Big Mama original. A larger-than-life matriarch, her role is socially centring as she holds it all together. She calls the shots, organises, keeps everyone in line and dispenses the rules when she has to.

Cancer needs to be needed. Part of nurturing is giving emotional nutrition and sustenance. The body part ruled by the sign of Cancer is the breasts. Symbolically she nurtures by feeding. She's particularly good when the little ones are still in the start-up phase before leaving the nest for independence.

Her quality is Cardinal, which brings the impulse to initiate – combined with the element Water, this results in the need to get all up in your emotional grill. If that's not received as she'd like, she'll retreat.

That hard exterior protectively harbours an empathic soul which picks up on all the emotions around her. She'll approach with caution, sideways, test the waters, test the ground, test your response to her. She's highly sensitive to rebukes and rebuttals. To feel and process she'll retreat into her inner shell, to curl up in its cosy comfort – and it *is* cosy, like a thick, woollen hooded onesie with built-in hot-water bottle. She'll come out of her shell in the safety zone of her home and with close ones.

Cancer is a foodie. She's an emotional comfort eater, with a well-stocked fridge. Her interest in food and nutrition can spill over to the sweet side with cakes. Reassuring meals like mama used to make are a regular feature on her menu when she's feeling tired, needs self-care or is lost in emotions.

The Cancerian is sentimental: if anyone still prints out and keeps a photo collection it will be her. Lineage is appreciated, from family and old friendships to antiques with a story. She has an instinct for collecting, some may say hoarding, keepsakes and memories. She'll remember childhood feelings and special times. If you are closely involved in her circle or are an expat who comes from her community, she'll be the first to take you under her wing with a view to keeping you there.

Cancer's interest is in the personal. She makes her connections by drawing ideas, concepts and actions together and finding the personal meaning in them. Abstractions are of little interest. This skill is fantastic in marketing, especially with online media, as authenticity and emotional connection trump detached, distant authoritarianism.

Cancer 'rules' small business. That initiating Cardinal energy is all about start-ups. Cancer has such a communal quality that she can be great at tapping into her network and putting all the parts together while building a business that profits everyone. Colleagues are like family and she likes to keep the same team.

Cancer is like a babbling brook. Ever noticed how your Cancerian friends tend to be quite chatty? They use speech mainly for connecting (rather than communicating), preferring to keep things light and away from dark topics so everyone feels relaxed and safe.

Classic Cancer
Frida Kahlo

Uncensored self-portraiture, a turbulent emotional history and creative expression of her feelings toward childbearing: that typified Frida Kahlo's Cancer traits. Also her stormy relationship.

She makes the classic Cancer list due to the particularly personal nature of the paintings she's so famous for. After a debilitating accident in her youth, she expressed both her physical as well as emotional feelings through art. The images are introspective self-portraits with symbols expressing her pain. Topics cover relationships, her anguish at her miscarriage and the prospect of never being able to have a child, her mixed heritage and her beloved homeland suffering through revolution. Children and mothering can be very close to the Cancerian's heart. Frida painted her own heart, blood, foetus and birth.

Cancer's impulse to bring together and support her family can flow into to the political arena if the situation calls for it. Frida was highly patriotic, choosing Mexican folk dress when she could have dressed like a European.

Cancer's rule over lineage and birth can be compared to the tree of life, a great symbol for this sign. Frida's painting 'Roots' depicts the artist supporting life, with roots and tendrils flowing from her body.

The Cardinal quality expressed by Frida was to reach out and creatively share her life and feelings.

Surviving the pitfalls of being a Cancer

Self-care
You form strong bonds with your immediate circle. You prefer to focus your emotional investment on a few, but don't let that come at a cost to your own wellbeing. Balance your care for others with healthy doses of self-care. Remember, a stronger you results in a better ability to share the overflow; don't be trapped into just looking after others. It's a beautiful quality, but if it gets out of balance it can go from caring to critical. It's not your natural way, but a 'me first' mindset can be healthy and is perfectly OK! Your glyph is a dual sign, so think of it as one for me, one for you – maintain a balance.

Choose friends wisely
You're a sensitive soul who empathises with everything going on around you. It's worth vetting those who want access to your comfortably feathered nest. Your love is one of the

most unconditional loves – invest it wisely. Go for the stable, grounded, affectionate and caring sorts. Remember, support isn't dependency.

Test new waters
Comfort zones are nice places to chill, but when your vitality is compromised, it's time to take some risks. Don't let fear of the unknown stop you from setting sail to new shores. What have you got to lose? Learn to recognise when it's time for the hermit crab to move into a more accommodating shell.

Feel your feels
Eating to ease your pain? Feel your feels... sit with them, don't react or seek refuge in a bowl of chocolatey comfort. If food becomes all-consuming, it's a sign something is out of balance. Identify what is lacking and fill your life with that, rather than filling up from your fridge. Sometimes we just don't recognise what we think is missing because it's not exactly in the form we expect. Take another look around and come up with at least three things you'd like in your life right now.

Calling in the one
Your kindred spirit is someone who can match your need for both emotional and physical security. You'd take a solid soul over gambling on a rockstar heartbreaker any day. (Although there is Cancerian Jerry Hall, who definitely chose the rockstar!) Cancerians care deeply and your beau will need to appreciate your ability to manage and organise at home. If you're interested in family make sure you're both on the same page with this one.

Cosying up to a Cancer

Family first
Cancers are all about family, so get personal and invite them into your home. Share your personal space and ask them about their family stories. Get nostalgic and look through old photos.

Nurture
Try a high tea in a cosy café or find out their favourite food and make it. They'll be blown away that you were so attentive. They'll want to look after you too: accept the hospitality.

Cancer in your chart
You might not be a Cancer, but you'll still feel the Cancer vibe

Look at your birth chart, and locate the area ruled by Cancer. In this area, you'll be emotionally sensitive, you'll need a familial, supportive environment and you'll be the glue that holds everyone you care about together.

House · If you have Cancer on the cusp of your 2nd House of income, resources and values, you gain from your ability to care and nurture. You'll value family and the personal approach that makes others feel emotionally nourished.

Cancer on the 8th House cusp of sex, shared resources and all things taboo will need to feel emotionally connected and safe to both enjoy sex as well as commit to any joint ventures such as children or investing money.

Planet · Venus in the sign of Cancer relates in a personal and nurturing way, needing lots of affection.

Mars in Cancer is motivated into action by family concerns. You'll function best when surrounded by support or even family.

Leo
I express

Proud · Creatively expressive
Vital · Charismatic · Strong
Brave · Fierce

JULY 23 – AUGUST 22
RULER Sun
ELEMENT Fire
MODE Fixed
HOUSE Associated with the 5th House
RULES The heart
PERSONALITY Extroverted
COLOUR Gold, yellow

Enter stage left! Leo's grand gestures are regal and radiant. Backed by her ruler the Sun, she emanates a warmth and VIP stance that says: 'All eyes on me!'. Dignified, graceful and full of vitality, this sign is here to learn about herself through creative expression.

Leo is sociable, loves parties and appreciates the collaborative output of others. She makes a great hostess, enjoying everything from block parties to lavish events.

Confidence is a key attitude with this sign. It's necessary for Leo to share her creativity. By exposing her abilities she makes herself vulnerable. As a natural self-promoter, Leo knows that if she doesn't believe in herself, why should anyone else?

You'd be forgiven for thinking Leos rule the hair. Often sporting great manes, they take pride in their presentation. It's the heart, though, pumping out life blood to the rest of our body, which is ruled by Leo. She's not only warm and loving, she tends to be loyal, passionate and romantic. Pride is a keyword, as are courage, honour and popularity.

Like the heart positioned in the centre of our body, she loves to be the centre of attention with an admiring entourage. Compliments will get you everywhere! No one welcomes them more than Leo; no one receives them so graciously. Watch her glow grow when you lavish her with praise.

The Sun represents ego consciousness, so Leo can be both enigmatic and egocentric. Taken to its extreme, it could be a nasty case of narcissism. More positively, it's a confidence that expresses itself with integrity.

In antiquity, the lioness preceded the lion as a symbol that defined strength and grace with an untameable heart. Leos are born leaders and resist social status and any kind of servitude. They know they're free to be what they want. They have a strong connection to their instincts and tend to act on them.

Leo has a direct line to her inner child and uses it to create, as well as play and have fun. Her drive is to share her creations with others in a spirit of generosity. Her natural creativity extends from fun and games to a love of children. (She's the lioness, remember?) Not only does she play with her cubs, she's the hunter who works with the group to bring home the dinner. For this reason Leo can turn from the pussycat to the fierce big cat if she needs to. She'll hold her ground in a power struggle and tends to do well in business and career, since she'll step up to the plate and go after what she wants.

Classic Leo
Charlize Theron

Charlize is our Leo poster girl due to her ability to triumph in various creative fields and take control of her career in a cutthroat industry.

Of all of the performing arts, Leo has a special place in her heart for dancing, and Charlize originally worked as a model to support her ambition to become a professional dancer.

Leo isn't afraid to throw a tantrum if she needs to vent. She's a Fire sign, after all. Fatefully, Theron's first manager met her in a bank where she was doing just that. A dramatic expression of frustration turned out to be what got the ball rolling in Tinseltown. Roar power!

Leos throw themselves wholeheartedly into their passions. Like the Sun, they keep shining and feeding off the warmth they get back in the form of love and applause.

Surviving the pitfalls of being a Leo

Loud and proud
As one particularly famous Leo puts it, 'Express yourself, don't repress yourself' (yes, Madonna is one of those fierce lionesses). Try different creative vehicles that allow you to shine and be well received. The classics are dance, drama and art, as well as physical activities like snowboarding and other sports. Leadership roles give you something to sink your teeth into as well as grow into. You're great front of house and make a super spokesperson.

Vet your audience
Compliments get anyone anywhere with you, Leo. You probably deserve the praise, but your ego is an easy side door in for the less scrupulous to mess with your heart. Be discerning. Do they have an agenda that is in line with your mutual interests? On the same note, arrogance can see you pass over those who could prove to be great supporters.

Where's my encore?
Leo, you easily attract attention with your natural exuberance and ability to get your point across with integrity and sincerity. Many other mere mortals struggle to unleash themselves as freely as you can, which can cause a backlash. If more restrained or repressed types get snarky, see if it's because they aren't able to express whatever you're expressing. Know what not to take personally – it tells you more about them and where they're at.

Shine from an internal frame of reference
Have you taken your natural flair for drama into a needy play for attention? If it seems unjustified and isn't getting you what you want, hit the reset button. Your star power comes from within so get centred and work it out from there.

Calling in the one
You're a Fire sign that burns with romantic passion and ardour. Any perfect partner will need to have the confidence to keep you enthralled, with no slacking off. Saying it with grand gestures of flowers, gondola tours, compliments and lots of

affection is a great start. If you're anything less than the apple of their eye, I suggest you say au revoir. You're a leader and like to run the show, so shared power is a must.

Cosying up to a Leo

Roll out the red carpet
Leos love to be recognised for what they share, either one-on-one or with the world. Let them know what you adore about them and make sure you mean it. Tell them every time you see them, they'll never tire of it!

Get the party started
Think 'show-pony/party girl' and plan accordingly. Leo loves live events, dressing up, glamming up and dancing.

Creative coupling
One of the classiest signs, Leo loves to help others polish up and look their best. Take them on a shopping makeover trip and let them work their magic on you.

Leo in your chart
You might not be a Leo, but you'll still feel the Leo vibe

Look at your birth chart, and locate the area ruled by Leo. In this area, you'll need to make grand statements, express yourself and retain creative control.

House · If Leo rules the 7th House of partnership you need your relationship to preserve the romance, to be treated like a queen and to have a significant other to be proud of. Watch out for drama!

Leo on the ascendant (1st House) knows how to make an entrance. You easily draw others to you immediately. Leadership may come easily to you, as you appear to fit the part.

Planet · Mars in Leo is motivated by fun and creativity. Your actions are assured and definitive.

Moon in Leo needs some drama in her life! You have a way of presenting yourself that draws attention and you'll feel at ease when you know you're number one.

♍ Virgo
I analyse

**Perfectionistic · Detail-orientated
Humble · Efficient · Helpful
Mind/body connection · Simplicity**

AUGUST 23 – SEPTEMBER 22
RULER Mercury
ELEMENT Earth
MODE Mutable
HOUSE Associated with the 6th House
RULES The intestines
PERSONALITY Introverted
COLOUR White, lilac, muted brown

The original minimalist, Virgo has razor-sharp editing skills, meaning she can bag-and-bin anything without practical purpose – she's able to analyse what is useful and worth keeping, with any excess deftly taken care of.

She's known for a habit of measuring everything (and everyone) against her inner ideal, then sets about making reality match as closely as possible. This has given her a reputation for perfectionism, and at its best, this quality comes across as cool, calm, confident and professional. Unbalanced, and at her worst, Virgo clings too tightly to the inner vision of perfection and is apt to hurl criticism at the space between ideal and reality. Both towards herself and others.

The urge to analyse just won't quit, and her ability to dissect with precision and attention to detail makes Virgo a perfect candidate for being a surgeon. Imagine those sutures!

In a similar way to this emotional and practical ability to edit, Virgo is a natural biological editor as the sign rules our intestines (and therefore the physical process of breaking down and assimilating nutrients from the digestive tract into the body, while discarding non-essentials). When out of balance, they can experience tummy upsets and digestive issues.

Luckily, Virgos have a keen interest in natural health, diet and exercise. They take care of their body and have an innate understanding of the mind/body connection.

Ruled by Mercury (the mind and nervous system), Virgo can be somewhat sensitive. Overthinking can lead to worrying and anxiety. But Virgo is also an Earth element: a Mercury ruler combined with Earth gives Virgo a solid, practical edge.

Virgo's strength is in developing knowledge and applying it in a practical way. This particularly applies to personal and emotional problems, as they are always striving to make inner order out of inner chaos. (This is reflected brilliantly by the tail on the Virgo symbol, which turns inwards.)

Accomplished and humble, this quiet achiever produces magical results in just about any area she puts her nimble mind to task. Focus on detail, strong work ethic and desire to serve are the keys to Virgo's impressive ability to manifest.

Earth also makes Virgo keen on routine and preparedness. She needs daily habits and rituals to set her course and her watch by. But she's no stick-in-the-mud. The sign is Mutable, meaning Virgos can be adaptable. She's also apt to surprise you with a deadpan gallows humour that will have you in stitches.

Classic Virgo
Elizabeth I of England

This Queen embodies classic Virgo traits. Virgos will always keep something back that's sacred for themselves. In this case, Elizabeth was known as the Virgin Queen – she retained her power by allowing suitors to visit, yet chose never to marry. The original meaning of Virgin had nothing to do with chastity and everything to do with belonging to oneself and no other. A Virgo's inner sanctum is a place you'll never enter.

Earth signs are hard workers, they know and respect how the world works. Elizabeth dutifully stepped up into her role, navigating a male-dominated world, and cleverly maintained her position, reigning for a mighty 44 years.

Presentation is everything to a Virgo. Their reserve can intimidate and create mystique. Shrewdly utilising the media of the day, Elizabeth branded herself through dramatic costume and striking portraiture.

Surviving the pitfalls of being a Virgo

Counteract the angst
Over-worrying is a classic Virgo trait. Some Virgos might take to blitz cleaning when their feelings are flying around, others turn to exercise. Virgos should always identify restorative ways to relax and clear any negative thoughts. Ideally, the relaxing activity will help you feel more earthed – think about gardening, getting active or simply taking time out with yourself. Breathe and give yourself a break from time-to-time, Virgo.

Find balance
The opposite sign to Virgo in polarity is Pisces. On the Virgo end we have extreme order, therefore on the other side is extreme chaos. When Virgo is exerting too much retentive control, bottled emotions tend to spill over. Find balance by incorporating some of the positive Piscean traits of surrender, creative chaos, non-judgment and emotional connection through vulnerability.

Keep it simple
Streamline, simplify and edit. Less is more. You're already good at this, but remember to play to your strength.

Calling in your perfect match
You need someone who'll appreciate you. You know how you like things. Suitors must respect your ways while encouraging you to share your private thoughts and feelings. Messy, unhygienic and unfocused people will fray your fine edges. Opt for a polished, refined bae – someone who knows all the right ways to behave when they meet your mother, or accompany you to a function.

Cosying up to a Virgo

Information is king
They'll be up in your grill wanting to know all the minutiae of how things work – they'll want the dates, times, ETAs, nitty gritty of who went where, what they ate, how they felt…

Make sure you fill them in and don't spare on the detail. They need it to make sense out of life, and feel nervous with only a vague big picture.

Mind your manners
Employ the old-fashioned 'rules'. Be early, showcase your manners. A little bit of praise goes a long way, too. Praise their work and work ethic, and loyalty. And let them know their attention to detail hasn't gone unnoticed. Politely make the first move.

Keep it clean
Talk cleaning products, efficiency, diet and nutrition… or filing! Get physical and talk about what makes a healthy body: it equals a healthy mind, after all. Swap workout app tips and ask exactly how many burpees it took to look so svelte. If in doubt you can't go wrong discussing work, work and more work.

Virgo in your chart
You might not be a Virgo, but you'll still feel the Virgo vibe

Look at your birth chart, and locate the area ruled by Virgo. In this area, you'll be organised, and interested in health and routines with great attention to detail.

House · If you have Virgo rising (on the cusp of the 1st House), you might notice a humble yet professional approach to life – you'll cut a clean, sharp image, ably putting your best foot forward in new situations. You'll apply the principles of health, organisation and attention to detail to life generally.

On the cusp of the 4th House representing the home you'll run a tight ship and actually enjoy cleaning, maintaining and arranging your home.

Planet · The action principle of Mars through a filter of Virgo will be practical and detail-oriented. They will find it hard to relax and always keep busy. Filing, forms and applications are a great way to the top for anyone with Mars in Virgo. Organising and logistics are ideal.

With Moon in Virgo you feel emotionally secure when your need for daily routine is met. You feel great satisfaction when your efforts to nurture and help are met with gratitude.

♎ Libra
I balance

Balanced · In harmony · Compromising · Charming Justice · Equal in relationships

SEPTEMBER 23 – OCTOBER 22
RULER Venus
ELEMENT Air
MODE Mutable
HOUSE Associated with the 7th House
RULES The kidneys
PERSONALITY Extroverted
COLOUR Pastels

Lovely Libra. Before Scorpio sidles up to touch base, Libra will want to set your scales. Say hello to blossom-carpeted picnics and pretty shades of soft pastels.

The sixth of twelve signs in the zodiac, Libra holds a mirror up to the 'other', and attempts to reduce the space between. Libra's greatest urge is to balance and harmonise opposites. The essential idea of equal balance is derived from the autumn equinox, when night and day find harmony as the northern hemisphere moves from summer to winter.

Harmony of proportion is the key to beauty in music, art, design and architecture. A strong Libran focus in a birth chart will point toward a natural disposition and ability in those areas. Many an interior decorator, makeup artist and architect are found in its ranks.

Socially, the initiating Cardinal nature of Libra presents as a drive to establish balance. Solutions that hit the most melodious chord with all parties involved are her speciality. Careers in law, negotiation and arbitration combine well with her intelligence and passion for mutually agreeable solutions. Libra always strives to hit that sweet spot. When reading any placements involving Libra, always apply this theory and you'll be halfway there.

The symbol for Libra is the scales, the only inanimate object in the zodiac. Inferred from this is their ability to operate from an impartial point of view, detached from primal nature.

Librans can appear flaky or indecisive, but they may just be avoiding conflict as they know the price of decision. They can see all sides of an argument and want to bypass the potential loss and perhaps anger expressed by the losing party. More sensitive signs prone to unquestioning loyalty, like Cancer, can feel unsupported by Libra's careful non-bias.

Opposite sign Aries is famous for stepping up in a fight as well as kicking off with a bit of rabble-rousing of her own. Ruled by Venus, Libra is a lover not a fighter, yet compelled by a pervasive drive for peace, she can't help but enter the fray. She's proved that great achievements in reconciliation are possible without uncivilised barbaric or bloody behaviour.

Classic Libra
Serena Williams

Tennis is a sport ruled by the genteel, polite sign of Libra. The greatest champion of the modern era is Serena Williams, with not only her Sun, but Mercury, Jupiter, Saturn and Pluto all in the sign of the scales.

Libra's urge to be partnered up sees Serena in a position of strength. She trained with her sister Venus, later competing with her in doubles matches. The two lived together, with Serena referring to Venus as her soulmate. Serena also channels the Libran ability to leave it on the court and go back to the perfectly balanced harmony of being best friends.

As an Air sign, Serena has a truly powerful mental game to achieve her outstanding wins. Air signs also place high value on education and Serena has helped build schools in Africa, as well as funded American schools for the underprivileged. As a classic peace-loving Libran, her other charity focus is combating violence. She's set up her own centres for rehabilitating victims and families of violent crime.

In interview, as well as responding to unfair or rude behaviour, Serena displays the diplomacy and charm that sets Librans apart, while still getting her message across loud and clear.

Surviving the pitfalls of being a Libra

Stand your ground
You bend yourself all sorts of ways in order to avoid conflict. Don't let bullies win: stand your ground. It's cool to say 'no' as well as to change your mind about a decision or agreement that's not right for you. Judge your relationships on how you feel when you've been with that person. If you're doing too much personal paddling to keep afloat, like a swan's feet swimming under the water, it may be time to say bye-bye.

Look under the surface
You thrive when around beauty and harmony, sometimes avoiding the deeper issues, or the ugly side of life. Be aware of remaining too much on the surface due to your finely tuned sense of refinement and need for keeping up appearances.

Pick your battles
Don't get caught up in others' dramas. Know which battles to give your energy to. You are a natural mediator, but you are not responsible for sorting out everyone's clashes. Pick your battles and apply your skills to a bigger cause where you can make a difference while enhancing your own life. If your own scales are tipping, check yourself before you wreck yourself.

Calling in your significant other
First and foremost, you are *the* sign of one-on-one partnership, so be sure potential partners are upfront with their intentions for commitment. Your special someone needs to be articulate as well as amenable to both collaboration and compromise.

You absolutely need evenness and fair resolution, so seek a partner that is as dedicated to that as you. Libra can feel social pressure to conform to standards, but choose your partner to match you, not your family, peers or expectations.

Cosying up to a Libra

Sugar rush
Librans just love, well… love. Impress them with an outing to the opera or a candlelit table by a busy promenade. Like all Air signs, they're social and need light, airy spaces to feel comfortable. Keep the champagne flowing. Oh, and sweets!

It's all about me, I mean you, I mean me
As the sign of 'the equal other', they'll want to know all about you, so show your best side first. Any activities that take two to tango will bring you together. Tennis, anyone? Collaboration is the name of the Libran game.

Libra in your chart
You might not be a Libra, but you'll still feel the Libra vibe

Look at your birth chart and locate the area ruled by Libra. In this area you'll require harmony, one-to-one time and equal relationships.

House · If Libra rules your 6th House of health and daily routine, any overt conflict will eventually lead to ill health. You need harmony and beauty both daily and at work to maintain your equilibrium and wellbeing. Often your best work is accomplished with a teammate.

Libra rising (1st House) attributes beauty to your outward appearance and charm to your initial interactions, and means you prefer company.

Planet · Planets in Libra function via the standard Libra filter. Mars in Libra considers others before acting. This principle is effective in a dynamic duo or on behalf of the other person in a win-win arrangement. Make love, not war!

Moon in Libra needs emotional peace, but has an innate ability to negotiate and tends to avoid conflict at almost any cost.

Scorpio
I transform

Transformative · Powerful · Intense
Secretive · Esoteric · Psychic · Deep

OCTOBER 23 – NOVEMBER 21
RULER Pluto
ELEMENT Water
MODE Fixed
HOUSE Associated with the 8th House
RULES The reproductive organs
and organs of elimination
PERSONALITY Introverted
COLOUR Deep purple, crimson, black

A sign says 'Caution, trespassers beware', yet the zodiac's bad girl is magnetic. It's time to go deep. Let's get metaphysical with the most notorious, dark and mysterious sign.

With the velvet-gloved touch of a cat burglar she'll lay bare your secrets and expose your weak spots. Mercifully, though, she'll take them to the grave. Fiercely loyal, Scorpio has a tribe vibe that I'd pick as first choice to have by my side. The same is expected in return. If she thinks your loyalty falls short, you'll be dead to her. Don't disappoint and never, ever betray.

Like her symbol, the scorpion, she protects herself with an armour, in her case one of mystery. Deep within lies a vulnerability and a fear of rejection, perhaps because Scorpio knows all the secrets.

Under her sign, seasonally speaking, the dark veil of northern-hemisphere night begins to lower over shortening days. It's no surprise that Halloween falls within her time of year. The image of the witch, with her dark clothing, cauldron and occult powers, often appeals to those with strong Scorpio placements. Scorpio beckons us into the underworld where the fabric of material reality is thin.

She's driven to dig into your hidden and taboo parts, and she gains a certain power from guarding a vault of others' indiscretions. One of her many superpowers includes a built-in BS detector. An intense, penetrating, laser-like stare sees straight through fake news, so don't even try any misdirection. Quite simply, she knows, so 'fess up.

Mystery, intrigue and forensics are very interesting to a part of this sign, even when they fill others with fear. She thrives on intensity, so shrinking violets and the superficial need not apply. Sex, death and the afterlife appeal to a curious nature that wants to find the edge and look beyond. Intrigued?

She appears as the second of the Water elements; think of Scorpio Water as sitting at the bottom of a deep, dark well. The surface may be still, but it's roiling beneath. Those with Sun or Moon in Scorpio tend to periodically slip into an inner emotional abyss to wrestle demons. Two potent images for Scorpio are the snake that sheds its skin and the phoenix who must burn to ashes before her life-enhancing powers of regeneration kick in. Like an alchemist who turns lead into gold, Scorpio evolves by transforming at a core emotional level.

As a Fixed sign, Scorpio doesn't easily let go. Her iron will may well have you peeling her fingers from whatever she's holding on to. Imperative in transformation is elimination, which is indicated by Scorpio's rulership over the sexual and reproductive organs. Imbalance can manifest itself in conditions that range from constipation to repeat urinary tract infections or problems involving the ovaries.

A strong drive for deep connection and intimacy is a characteristic of the way she operates from the sacral chakra. When Scorpio is ready to leave a relationship it often seems sudden. However, her thinking often goes on under the surface. She waits until the relationship is truly dead before leaving. Remember, she doesn't let go easily!

Classic Scorpio
Katy Perry

Katy Perry has not only her Sun in Scorpio, but her Moon, Pluto, Mercury and Saturn, making her an uber-Scorpio. That's a lot of planets in one sign, which means a particularly strong emphasis on the Water element as well as the Fixed quality. Water is all about connectivity and Scorpio is about the deepest, most transformative kind. To *really* connect we need to drop the armour and expose ourselves emotionally. It calls for vulnerability, and Katy is all about vulnerability. 'You can be right or you can be loved, I just want to be loved,' she once said in an interview.

Issues of power and the reclaiming of it are addressed in songs like 'Roar' and 'Power'. Typically Scorpio in outlook, Katy says she's 'stronger from the struggle'. Scorpios are born with hardwired survival instincts. Katy sees herself as a dark horse. This powerful sign is built to continually regenerate, transform and survive. Fixed signs like Scorpio have staying power.

Surviving the pitfalls of being a Scorpio

Trust issues
It's important for you to trust others, yet often you find yourself on the back foot. Be mindful of who you take into your inner sanctum. References and a background check would be right up your alley. On the other hand, it's important to maintain an open and light approach when meeting and getting to know others, so you don't inadvertently create the scenarios you fear.

Own your stuff
Basic psychological theory suggests that rejecting strength or Scorpio traits in others often means you're rejecting those traits within yourself. Attraction can function in the same way. Work through it and reclaim who you are.

Calling in the one
You'll be bored super-fast if anyone lets you walk all over them. You need to meet your match to make it last. Your perfect ten will have to score high in EQ and want to cultivate an intimate, private and deep connection. Forget the bad boy or girl and go for a solid contender who makes you feel safe and secure. They need to support you as much as you know you support the ones you love. Most of all you need to be able to trust them 100%.

Cosying up to a Scorpio

Confide in me
Let them in. Scorpio is a Water sign; they want and need both emotional and psychic connection, so share your feelings, fears and desires to build that bond.

Mystery tour
Explore the mysteries – attend a workshop on the metaphysical, or visit a tarot reader. We all inherently have extra sensory perception, but Scorpio is the most curious about these realms.

Prove your mettle
Themes of power and dominance are inferred by Scorpio's planetary ruler Pluto. To match them you must stand up to them, as they'll poke, prod and push your boundaries to see not only what you're made of, but if you're worth it. Show them they can trust you with their secrets.

Scorpio in your chart
You might not be a Scorpio, but you'll still feel the Scorpio vibe

Look at your birth chart and locate the area ruled by Scorpio. In this area you'll be a deep-diver, and you'll need to periodically regenerate and transform. Areas in the birth chart ruled by Scorpio are where intense experience occurs.

House · The 10th House of career demands transformation and passionate experience – such as working in a hospital ER.

Scorpio ruling the ascendant (1st House) is particularly magnetic and provocative. She holds her cards close to her chest and is attracted to natural mysteries.

Planet · Planets in Scorpio express their function acutely and powerfully: they want to rip through anything superficial.

Mercury in Scorpio frowns at small talk, is a natural researcher and is perhaps a little suspicious. Your secrets are safe with her.

Mars in Scorpio acts with energy and strong will; she'll never give up a fight. She has the grit and staying power to achieve fiercely held ambitions. If you have Mars in Scorpio, be sure the goal is worthy of your dedication.

Sagittarius
I see

Philosophical · Visionary · Independent · Enthusiastic · Honest · Optimistic

NOVEMBER 22 – DECEMBER 21
RULER Jupiter
ELEMENT Fire
MODE Mutable
HOUSE Associated with the 9th House
RULES The hips, thighs and buttocks
PERSONALITY Extroverted
COLOUR Flame blue, orange

Gypsy, philosopher and clown all at once, Sagittarius has her sights set on the next adventure in mind, body or spirit. She sets her course for excitement, hoping to find something larger than herself. No belief system is left unexplored in her quest for expansion and self-development.

Her sharp, flaming arrows of radical honesty catch you off-guard: they're designed to be shot into the darkness, lighting the horizon with their fire. She's open and candid, and her gift is to tell it like she sees it. This is the essence of her intuition.

Expansion is the impulse Sag brings to just about every area of life. What begins as a casual game of tennis becomes the zeal to dominate at Wimbledon, and a trip to the beach becomes a mission to save the whales – any story can become a tall tale in the blink of an eye. Exaggeration only *bends* the truth, it doesn't break it, right? She wants to get her point across and, with Sag, size matters. Her sign rules largesse, and she likes the 360-degree, all-seeing viewpoint from which she can pull together random concepts then work out how they fit together in the big picture. Mountains and high places appeal.

She's a Mutable sign, so she'll always deliver something new and over the top, whether it's her belief systems or her look. Sagittarius doesn't do 'subtle' or halfway. Expect change, constant motion and attention-grabbing excess.

Seemingly born under a lucky star, Sagittarius is ruled by the charmed planet Jupiter. Naturally in tune with the power of positive thinking and affirmation, she spots the silver lining in any cloud. She thinks things will go well – and most often they do. Even misadventure is seen in a positive light, because she'll be so excited at having experienced, and most importantly learned, something new. Saggies are the least likely sign to suffer from or stay feeling low too long. Even if she stumbles, her attitude may be one of curiosity, interest or excitement ('Oh great, now I can understand how awful this is for everyone, I totally get it!'). In response, she may seek the answer and antidote in the nearest self-help or yoga class. Next she'll be administering her cure to all and sundry. Sagittarians make natural candidates for medical careers due to their academic leanings combined with an impulse to liberate their compadres. When Dr Sag's positive attitude focuses in on healing, the outcome is usually a win.

She makes an excellent coach as well as salesperson due to her enthusiasm and can apply spin to just about anything. Marketing or trend-forecasting suit her well. We all have our unique role to play in this life. Sag has the gift of scouting ahead of the pack before bringing back her observations. This sign rules large in media and publishing; it tends to be popular, catches attention and knows just what to do when anything comes her way. Working in travel or with foreign cultures, if not overseas, is a no-brainer. As long as it expands her world, allows her abundant energy to work for her and gives her freedom combined with flexibility, she's in.

As a seeker of knowledge and the ultimate truth, Sag can be a perpetual student or become the seasoned professor living the academic dream.

Sagittarius is the third and final Fire sign and her glyph is an arrow. In astrology, arrows symbolise energy that needs external expression. This energy often translates into an upbeat enthusiasm that catches and spreads like a wildfire. But for all that confidence, swagger and love of the thrill of the chase, she can back away from intimacy and commitment when one-on-one. Freedom is her first love.

After building tension in the bow, the arrow released flies out at breakneck speed. Ability to fire rapidly while hitting dead centre is one of Sagittarius's skills.

Once she views her work as done or her surroundings lose their sparkle, stand back as Sag takes an Olympic-sized leap into new ranges to roam. She'll set goals that are so far in the distance they seem unrealistic to those around her, but the challenge to push herself past limits is exciting and motivating.

Sagittarius can be cerebral, yet her symbol, the centaur, is half-horse, meaning her body brings her back down to earth and into balance. The human half represents the female intellect harnessing male strength. The double nature of this sign means Sag can integrate both body and mind to move in unison.

Classic Sagittarius
Miley Cyrus

Sagittarius lets it all hang out. The most transparent sign, she is almost bulletproof to the opinions of others. In fact, the ability to smash through boundaries is in this sign's DNA. Once she finds her mission in life, not much deters her.

Miley wins the coming-out-of-the-century award. The spectacular leap she made to put distance between her childhood and tween years and into her young adult phase seemed extreme because it was so authentic and honest.

Miley's antics, like those of many Sagittarians, may deflect from what she has to say. They also remind us not to take ourselves or the disapproval of others too seriously. It's a paradox to help you catch yourself out and liberate you from assumptions and beliefs that you've internalised.

Taylor Swift deserves a mention as another classic Sag, down to her enormous success, girl-next-door authenticity and continued rapid growth. She's classically goofy as well as unrestrained physically. Sagittarians move their bodies around a lot and have very expressive faces. In her famous song 'Shake it Off' Swift encouraged everyone not to care what others think about them.

Surviving the pitfalls of being a Sagittarius

Lucky strikes
Like the strike of a match, your intuition is responsive and immediate. This is a key part of your intelligence and modern-mystic genius. Get to know how instinctive information comes to you so you can recognise and heed it. Is it in your body as a feeling or words, or is it an image that comes to mind? How is it different to daydreaming or thoughts? The more conscious you become of it, the clearer it will become, letting you make the right moves on the go with no break in your flow.

Perfect your aim and give it a red-hot go
Versatility as well as an all-round interest in life can leave you as a jack of all trades, master of none. I know it's hard, but choose a vehicle to drive further than just once around the track.

Find your platform… and your tact!
You're an inspired speaker whose prophetic words often come straight from your higher mind to your mouth, bypassing your brain. Filter it just enough so that people don't switch off.

Calling in the one
Watch for jealous, possessive and dominating partners: your freedom-loving sign attracts them. A special someone needs to be a great friend first before becoming a great partner. Vet them like you would your next course, ideology or travel adventure. Your intuition will let you know the right answer, even if it's not what you'd like to hear! The one for you is comfortable with your need for freedom and new scenes. They'll need to respect your mind and the broad range of experiences you crave. If you can learn something from them, even better. Like every other aspect of your life it's important to aim high and far beyond what you think your limits are.

Cosying up to Sagittarius

Bring the inspiration
Being a Mutable Fire sign, Sag needs exposure to fresh ideas to stimulate their mind and keep those flames of inspo burning. Take them to places or events where they'll learn something.

Just horsing around
Sagittarius rules comedy. They'll laugh at everything, and can come out with some great one-liners and observations. Take them out to a comedy night, play charades or just get their fire lit with your own hilarity. If all else fails, laugh at their jokes!

Born free
Sagittarius loves to move, especially in open spaces. They love nature, so plan a hiking and camping trip and bear in mind exotic locations are likely to be on the bucket list. Most importantly, make sure they know they're free to be themselves: this don't-fence-me-in type will bolt at the first sign of restriction.

Sagittarius in your chart
You might not be a Sagittarius, but you'll still feel the Sagittarius vibe

Look at your birth chart and locate the area ruled by Sagittarius. In this area you'll need freedom to explore, plus you'll have to search for meaning as well as room for expansion.

House · If Sagittarius rules the cusp of your 10th House, your career and public image will be upbeat and philosophical: you could make a decent politician, self-help guru or promoter of a cause.

Your 12th House cusp with a Sagittarian overlay indicates an expansive and inspirational dream life. Teaching in 12th House areas such as meditation would suit your abilities.

Planet · Mercury in the sign of Sagittarius is a positive mind: you'll be hungry for knowledge yet can sometimes seek too much information before making conclusions.

Venus in Sagittarius is attracted to funny, athletic or intellectual types. You know a Venus Sag is flirting when they start moving about, taking up space and throwing out joke after joke.

Capricorn
I use

Responsible · Authoritative
Ambitious · Persevering · Realistic
Achieving · Dutiful

DECEMBER 22 – JANUARY 19
RULER Saturn
ELEMENT Earth
MODE Cardinal
HOUSE Associated with the 10th House
RULES The knees, skeletal system and teeth
PERSONALITY Introverted
COLOUR Black, dark brown

She's bossy, because she *is* the boss. The Cardinal quality of Capricorn is seen in the upstanding horns of its symbol, the goat – it says, 'Let's forge ahead'.

Capricorn, the sign with the masterplan, wants no less than to scale the tallest heights. The most dignified and respectable sign on the block, she sets her sights on accomplishment and status. She's not one to waste time on showiness, preferring to work hard and quietly build an empire.

A traditionalist at heart, Capricorn has no interest in reinventing the wheel. Results-driven, economical and precise, she'll build on what's been proved to work in the past, then develop it and put it to use. Her leadership skills create a desire to systematise and structure. She wants things to work on a grand scale for the larger good. Associated with large corporations, Capricorn is drawn to high-level management roles. She wants a big impact for her effort and won't waste time on trivialities.

Capricorn is associated with time and limitations thanks to its rulership by the planet Saturn. Saturn's influence suggests Capricorn has an innate understanding of time as well as what is humanly possible to achieve in one hour, year or lifetime. She'll eye a challenge, create a plan then set to task on achieving her goal. She plays the long game. She'll ignore distractions and laugh in the face of procrastination. Sheer endurance and the ability to thrive in tough conditions can see her triumph long after others have lost pace.

Cap's got grit. If it wasn't hard won, Capricorn doesn't really appreciate it. She *likes* to work hard and maybe even suffer a little to produce results. She wants to pay her dues and earn the honour of respect and authority – and she's known for her reliability and responsibility.

She's a conservative sign, preferring established fashion labels that display old-school luxury, status and that coveted success. Capricorn knows people judge: what others think is important.

While the Cap symbol is a depiction of the mythical sea goat, the glyph actually represents the goat's nimble and sure foot atop the tail of a fish. This steady-going material girl often comes from humble beginnings before working her way up. It's certain she'll end up higher on the hill than where she began. The fish tail in the glyph can symbolise the place you begin, while the goat's hoof brings to mind steps up a mountain driven by inner fortitude and intuition.

Combining the concepts of time and ascent, Capricorn tends to improve with age. She's already a mature mini-boss when young, often preferring the company of older people she can respect and learn from. She knows patience and persistence pay off, so later life can see this silver fox coming into her own while others flounder along the way.

Physically, Capricorn rules the skeletal system. Capricorns are rigid, so any knee or joint problems suggest more flexibility, or even yielding, is needed to proceed. Draw on Capricorn's polarity of Cancer to soften or balance. Capricorns find it hard to take time off, but for their own wellbeing they should recognise when it's time to withdraw for some R&R. Too much burden and not enough support can cause issues: share the load.

The Cardinal quality of Capricorn mirrors the 'try, fail, try again' approach. Just get started and take it from there. So many successful people seem to have suddenly 'made it' easily by the time we hear about them, but it's usually taken years of hard work and many stumbles to arrive. That's the Capricorn quality right there.

Classic Capricorn
Michelle Obama

Michelle Obama embodies quite a few classic Capricorn traits, namely her stalwart ascent to the top from essentially humble beginnings, while maintaining masterful elegance throughout. She's a take-charge woman we can all rely on.

Capricorns are the most likely to use maxims and statistics to lend authority and validity to their words, so here are a few of Michelle's own classic Capricorn quotes you could adopt yourself.

'Always stay true to yourself and never let what somebody says distract you from your goals.' And: 'The only limit to the height of your achievements is the reach of your dreams and your willingness to work hard for them'. Classic Capricorn.

Surviving the pitfalls of being of a Capricorn

Status anxiety
Our society judges on income and status, with the first question upon meeting a new person often being: 'What do you do?' As an ambitious Capricorn, remember, you will get there. In the meantime, the journey, both personal and professional, is just that: a journey. Keep quality people in your life that value you for what's on the inside, not just the car you drive.

Workaholics anonymous
It can be lonely in that penthouse suite, and the long winding path to get there often is, too. Capricorns can be workaholics, willing to forgo fun to get the job done. Depression is associated with your sign so keep your tanks full and insist on a good work/life balance or that long-haul plan may encounter turbulence. Check in with yourself to make sure you're not burying any problems under piles of work or avoiding the personal side of life. These things take practise to master too.

Find your other half
Capricorn, you love an older, wiser type who can teach you the ways of the world, and if they have status of their own, that will be right up your street. Make sure there is room in the

relationship for you to grow in your own right. Your sign is ruled by Saturn, which points to your great awareness of boundaries. Be sure to enforce them in your relationships the way you're able to at work. If it's not ideal, then say so. The other half of a power couple could be great, or go for a softer soul who nurtures and soothes you when you're deep in the role of provider.

Cosying up to a Capricorn

Get formal
They love formal events, frocking up and blinging up – with real diamonds, of course. Take them to a ball or opera. They're a social sign and love to collect contacts, so get out and about.

Get grit
Being an Earth sign, Capricorn is practical and applies knowledge as she learns it. If you're going to talk the talk, they'll want to see you walk the walk. No sign will bat for you as hard as a Cap when they notice your grit and determination.

Capricorn in your chart
You might not be a Capricorn, but you'll still feel the Capricorn vibe

Look at your birth chart and locate the area ruled by Capricorn. In this area you'll be responsible, traditional and ambitious, striving for success in the long-term.

House · Capricorn on the 7th House cusp of partnership will want a traditional set-up with a sensible and reliable partner.

On the cusp of the 9th House (higher education and travel), she'll need certification from a well-regarded institution. A slowly-slowly approach may be taken to education, developing philosophies and expanding the mind.

Planet · Mercury in the sign of Capricorn indicates an orderly way of thinking that structures information into useable strategies and solutions.

Mars in Capricorn directs energy toward achievement. Many successful people over the years have this placement.

Aquarius
I know

**Humanitarian · Unconventional
Innovative · Intellectual · Rebellious
Detached**

JANUARY 20 – FEBRUARY 18
RULER Uranus
ELEMENT Air
MODE Fixed
HOUSE Associated with the 11th House
RULES Ankles, shins and calves
PERSONALITY Extroverted
COLOUR Electric blue, neon

Aquarius: radical, original and independent. She's an Air sign, and expresses her wonderfully unconventional qualities through thought and communication. Aquarius runs high voltage, with a sparky, livewire magnetic quality.

The glyph for Aquarius is two zigzag lines which represent both moving water and energy or frequency. Her image is the water bearer, positioned on a cloud high above the Earth. From her great height she pours the rain of knowledge onto the masses below. Aquarian water nourishes new life in terms of ideas and consciousness.

The role of Aquarius as the harbinger of change is to question the status quo. A sharp shake ensures societal structures of the sort built by earthy Capricorn don't become calcified or outdated. No one sleeps on an Aquarian's watch! In fact, her style is anything but subtle when the shock of the new is needed to wake the complacent. She keeps things fresh, as all-moving water does. Symbolised by the negative ions – cool, calm and bright after a storm – she brings clarity and awareness.

Aquarius cares: not so much about you personally, but about how you fit into the wider social structure. She's all about the intersection, the commonalities we share, and how she can arrange them so we can all thrive. Often uncomfortable one-to-one, Aquarius directs herself toward the rights of the individual while reverse-engineering via the larger group.

She is at her best when she has a cause to support. She'll be saving the whales, marching for peace and lobbying the government, but human rights are her first love. She'll be attracted to larger organisations or institutions that mirror her beliefs. This could be political movements, publishing, syndicated television or, of course, the ultimate Aquarian invention, the worldwide web.

Aquarius is future-oriented and often prophetic, and loves sci-fi. The field of science, chemical engineering or even larger-scale, socially oriented architecture and planning draw this erudite thinker.

Aquarius is Fixed Air, which lends staying power to her ideas, ideals and vision. She sings 'I did it my way,' while marching to the beat of her own drum. (Often so far ahead she'll be considered a bit bonkers by other less visionary types.)

Air signs can be detached, and Aquarius displays this quality more than any other, which contributes to maintaining her unique position on life, the Universe and, well, everything.

Classic Aquarius
Oprah Winfrey

Oprah ticks so many of the Aquarian boxes: group orientation; challenging the status quo; altruism; and friendship, to name a few. Aquarius is known as an inventor, and as an Air sign her speciality is ideas and communications.

Having the Sun, Mercury and Venus in change-maker sign Aquarius, Oprah has achieved elevated success by working with the expression inherent in her sign. She's moved from being a people pleaser to being authentic and pleasing herself.

Interestingly, another wildly successful talk show host is Ellen DeGeneres, who also happens to have her Sun and Venus in Aquarius. Aquarius is born to speak to the populace and move mountains by connecting intellectually and reorganising things that need changing. For Aquarius, knowledge is indeed power.

Aquarius will champion the underdog and fight inequality. Friendship is also so important to Aquarians and Oprah is all about that, too. Oprah and long-time partner Stedman Graham have been engaged since 1992! Yes, Aquarians like to have their space and do things their way.

Surviving the pitfalls of being Aquarius

Stay grounded
Being so cerebral can come at the price of becoming lost in the airy spaciousness of your mind. Stay grounded by dropping into your body and your feelings. Mindfulness practice is perfect for you.

Rebel with a cause
Every worthy cause needs a brilliant thinker and every brilliant thinker needs a worthy cause. If it lights you up and engages your higher power, volunteer, spread the word or even go full-time pro for a humanitarian or eco cause. This will channel your abundant energy and focus your intellect.

Looking for a spark
Shared interests and peer connections are vital or you'll go your separate ways. A partner who has some domestic ability and can bring warmth to your home will be a great attribute. You can be free to pursue your interests and entertain, as well as have a home and partnership to help ground you. A bright spark who can not only keep up with you intellectually, but also stimulate your mind is essential.

Cosying up to Aquarius

Friends first
Aquarius is associated with peers, so friendship is highly valuable. They're loyal cohorts and appreciate the space they gain within friendship as opposed to traditional partnerships. So friend up, give them space, connect intellectually and find a common cause to share if you want to cosy up to this high-vibe water-bearer.

Clarity
Open and honest Aquarius prefers clear communication. If in doubt just ask and always put your cards directly on the table or they'll push you out of the club.

Aquarius in your chart
You might not be Aquarius, but you'll still feel the Aquarian vibe

Look at your birth chart, and locate the area ruled by Aquarius. In this area you'll be on the vanguard, plus you'll require a lot of space while seeking out groups of like-minded peers.

House · Aquarius ruling your ascendant (1st House) will give you a humanitarian outlook on life, where you'll seek to express yourself with diverse people from all walks of life. You'll present as sparky and possibly erratic. You'll seek to apply a unique signature to everything you do.

Ruling the 10th House of career and public image, Aquarius signifies unusual professions, cutting edge or scientific. There may also be a humanitarian aspect to your career.

Planet · Moon in Aquarius lends an objective ability to the emotional life. You're nurtured by friendships and need space to process your emotions. You'll have to work at feeling your feels rather than intellectualising them or detaching.

Venus in Aquarius appreciates unique people from all walks of life. With the sign of the socialite, she loves making new connections and exchanging ideas. Love may be long-distance, detached or unconventional.

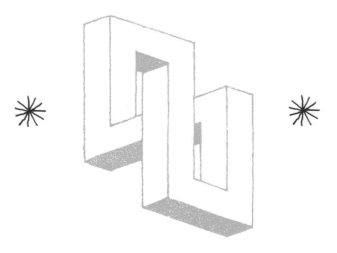

Pisces
I believe

Creative · Sensitive · Romantic
Empathetic · Glamorous · Intuitive
Open boundaries

FEBRUARY 19 – MARCH 20
RULER Neptune
ELEMENT Water
MODE Mutable
HOUSE Associated with the 12th House
RULES The feet
PERSONALITY Introverted
COLOURS Metallics, purple, millennial pink

The veil between this world and the next one is drawn away as the siren song of Pisces softens the hard, harsh lines of conscious reality. She's ethereal and prefers life in the spiritual waters of that place where dreams are made.

Highly sensitive, she picks up on subtleties in a way that almost seems mystic. Pisces notices micro expressions and learns a lot from tone of voice – she knows more than what you think you're saying. She's exquisitely in touch with detail. Pisces can spot a potential tryst or Tinder match at twenty yards – straight up, there's no hiding anything from her.

She has a yearning to transcend this physical Earth and float away. It can be a battle for her to keep her head above water in the daily grind. It's not exactly that she has a death wish, but her inner voice is constantly telling her to give in, to let go of the ego or collection of ideas, thoughts and memories we identify with as our 'self'.

She has an innate understanding of oneness, the idea that we are all connected and not as separate as we appear. Constricted by reality, she wants her boundaries to erode and dissolve. Pisces is an escape artist. She finds ways to exit mundane reality by using her imagination to daydream; she might become lost in art, or turn to substances like drugs and alcohol. Pisces is the sign of addiction. At her best she finds inspiration to do something greater than herself, discovering true insights and creating great art – many a genius did their best thinking while sleeping or daydreaming. At her worst, she finds escape through destructive means and begins to rely on that method. The key is to find healthy sustainable ways of finding bliss.

The symbol for Pisces is two fish, each swimming in opposite directions. This Mutable sign's element is Water. Due to Pisces' dual nature, she's highly adaptable and experiences the world through emotions. One fish swims upstream while the other goes with the current. She's highly changeable and versatile, a slippery fish that won't be pinned down.

Her soft heart, empathy and compassion are legendary. Very likely to apply unconditional love, she's driven to help relieve suffering and pain motivated by the potential she sees in every soul. Her great sensitivity endows her with a special connection to animals. And she makes an excellent therapist or spiritual guide. Any career in which she can express her sensitivity and empathy will suit.

Pisces can live in the moment, be playful and extremely responsive, as well as glamorous with an elusive, illusory quality. Paradoxically, she finds it hard to let go when she's given her heart in love. Very impressionable, Pisces can be influenced by those around her. To protect herself, she will go with the flow and ride the waves rather than be battered by resistance.

Classic Pisces
Ruby Rose

Model turned VJ, turned DJ, turned TV host, turned actress, turned writer, Ruby Rose is a classic Pisces. Mutable signs are flexible, have a responsive nature and are often multi-talented.

Ruby dramatically expresses the fluctuation that her dual symbol represents. Her ability to blur gender lines as well as cross career channels seems effortless. When it comes to applying the concept of fluidity, Water-babe Pisces takes the prize.

Ruby has credited her growing popularity to expressing who she really is rather than toeing the line. She's out and proud. and that's what you call embracing your sign's superpowers!

Surviving the pitfalls of being a Pisces

Top up
You tend to be the least assertive and most self-sacrificing of the signs. It's noble to help others, but your glass needs to be full before you fill someone else's. Keep an eye on your levels and make sure to take time out to top up your reserves.

The path to oneness
Find a healthy and sustainable way to reach a higher ground. You need methods of 'losing' yourself and transcending the everyday. Creative outlets tick the boxes and you'll build skills along the way – perhaps even combine it with your profession. Illustration, fine art, music or photography are all great choices. Get into the ocean and swim, or explore meditation and mystical philosophies.

Leave the soap operas to TV
You're an emotional sponge whose power is to pick up on nuances. This great quality also trips you up: your radar is so tuned into fine emotional detail that molehills can turn into mountains. Learn to know what's worth letting flow by you.

Calling in the one
Pisces, you want nothing less than a soulmate – someone you can believe in. Make sure they're available emotionally and can provide the depth and romance you crave. Find someone who is both an anchor and a sheltered port to dock when the seas are stormy. You fare well with a partner who is very solid and grounded, yet who can appreciate your own creative flights and dreams. You are drawn to artists and those who need saving, but it's advisable to attend to them in your professional not personal realm: keep it as a civic duty or special interest or hobby. Home and heart needs to be stable if you are to meet your own potential and maintain an even keel.

Cosying up to a Pisces

Love for the lover
Pisces is sensitive, so tread lightly. Give them lots of love and validation, whether you're just friends or maybe more. In particular, validate those super-perceptive feelings: go in for emotional closeness and connection.

Get creative
Appeal to their need for creative escape by dressing up, role playing, or going to live gigs or cool art shows. Cover them in glitter and take them to a music festival where they can lose their sense of the everyday and connect with the communal scene.

Share the 'helper's high'
Pisces loves working in harmony with others on collabs for a higher purpose. Hack your body's natural feelgood pharmacy together by inducing the 'helper's high', dopamine, and volunteering your time to those less fortunate.

Pisces in your chart
You might not be a Pisces, but you'll still feel the Pisces vibe

Look at your birth chart and locate the area ruled by Pisces. In this area you'll be sensitive, compassionate and creative, and lack solid boundaries.

House · Pisces on the cusp of your 6th House influences day-to-day work, routine and health. To keep your wellbeing ticking along you'll need to dream and let go – meditation, or losing yourself in music, could help. Work involves compassionate service or creativity, and you may have trouble saying no.

If Pisces influences your 2nd House of money and values, this suggests your ability to earn coin comes from your compassionate and creative abilities.

Planet · Moon in Pisces makes you a sensitive, romantic sort. Art will soothe your soul and you may harbour artistic talent.

Venus through the filter of Pisces' oneness is open to new people and can find beauty in everyone.

III. Elements

The four elements are Fire, Earth, Air and Water. Each element describes basic psychological traits of human behaviour and are often seen as types of energy. There are three signs for each of the four elements, and the expression of each element can be observed in many ways: in body type, hair texture and food preferences, among others. But, more importantly, they relate to a person's 'vibes', their approach to life's challenges and their characteristics.

To identify the elements in your birth chart, look at the position of the planets within each sign, and then the element of that sign. Focus on the sign the Sun and other personal planets are in first – what elements are these signs? Then move on to the outer planets. Ideally you'll see a balance of planets spread out evenly among the signs, and therefore a balance of elements. But the chances are you'll find that at least one element may be lacking or overrepresented in your chart. This imbalance brings its own challenges – you may be strong at expressing one element and weaker at expressing another.

Merely knowing the balance of elements in your birth chart (or someone else's chart) will give you an understanding of your (or their) approach to life.

Fire
Intuition

Aries · Leo · Sagittarius

**Intuitive · Energetic · Confident
Enthusiastic · Passionate · Boisterous**

Fire types perceive through intuition, prophetic vision and forecasting. With just a little information, they can leap into life's potentials and outcomes. They often live in the future rather than being present in the now.

Fire is an energy of the spirit. It's identified by a joyful, high-energy, wild vibe, with lots of movement and confidence. Fire types are very positive and self-assured, and full of bravado. They're stimulating to be around, they're direct and generally quite honest (sometimes brutally so). They naturally attract and enjoy attention. Their responses are speedy and assertive, but they become bored quickly and soon need to move on to the next stimulus.

Highly idealistic, Fire types can be naive and innocent. They can also be restless: in a tug-of-war, they start off strong, then throw in the towel and go off in search of something else to keep themselves amused.

Avoiding restrictions, they can be tripped up by the limits of material reality. In terms of the physical body, they can suffer injuries. This can bring Fire types back 'down to Earth' when they're out of balance. As the most psychologically different from Earth types, Fire types need Earth to ground them in the present. Air types are a good match, as they provide new ideas for Fire types to respond to and feel encouraged by.

Too much Fire in your chart

You're not shouting, you're just debating passionately! Highly enthusiastic about what you believe in, you find meaning in just about everything. Like a blazing inferno, you're a rush of kinetic energy, literally moving physically and feeling a need to roam.

You'll want to burn the candle at both ends with all that energy inside, but you're likely to exhaust your natural reserves, since there's not enough of the other elements to balance your output and exuberance. Careful you don't burn out!

Anger, impatience and riding roughshod over quieter, more sensitive types can result from an imbalance of Fire. Though often an overabundance of an element produces the reverse effect: since Fire seeks attention, too much of this element can create high spirits and a confidence within that you don't express externally. The outcome is you won't seek attention and can appear shy.

Physically, inflammation or issues around heat may be a problem for you. Avoid heating/stimulating foods like chilli, coffee and alcohol. Since Fire is already energising, adding more of the same can make problems worse, so avoid deep-fried, oily food, as well as sour flavours. Stay calm by eating fresh, raw foods. Drink lots of water to keep your engine cool.

Not enough Fire in your chart

Not enough Fire may result in a lack of inspiration, motivation and joy, which can lead to low energy, low vitality, low feelings or even depression.

Fire lends a certain confidence, so a lack of it can result in shyness. Conversely, if you have insufficient Fire you might go out of your way to seek attention, becoming a performer.

Digestion can be sluggish, so bring in stimulants that have a Fire element, like chilli or coffee. And soak up lots of sun, light and warmth. Intense exercise, like running, builds Fire. Power yoga, like Ashtanga, also helps.

If you lack Fire in your chart, import it! Invite Fire types into your life to teach you how to live with a high-energy outlook.

Earth
Sensation

Taurus · Virgo · Capricorn

Practical · Grounded · Cautious
Enduring · Sensuous · Dependable

Earth types understand the world through their senses. If it can be sensed, it's real. Less inclined towards airy conceptual ideas, they seek purpose and practicality, they are grounded and live in the present.

Coherence is important to Earth types – they like to have a plan and know what's happening. If the future is unknown or uncertain, they can feel anxiety and insecurity, becoming controlling. They prefer habits, rituals, and at all times they seek to establish security.

The material world is their playground (that could be food, nature or even money). It's understandable, since the Earth element literally relates to Mother Earth and the manifest physical realm. It rules civilisation, economics and finance, and it rules the way we apply value, both tangible and spiritual.

Earth types embody and live by their own values. They will happily plod the slow, practical and methodical route to building up resources and money, and achieving their goals.

In terms of health, Earth types have a robust constitution, a clear, waxy complexion and a solid appetite. They're more in tune with their bodies than the Air, Fire and Water types thanks to their connection with the senses. Earth signs often have an innate understanding of natural medicine as well as the healing potential within their own bodies.

Too much Earth in your chart

Too much Earth results in becoming stuck, inflexible and set in your ways. Emotionally, depression can set in if there's insufficient Fire to lift the spirits. Change can be difficult and feared. Letting go as part of change can also be challenging for you. You'll find it hard to move with the times, and can become fixated on the material realm. Your reaction times will be slow, but your persistence and patience will be super-strong. Steadfast and loyal, commitment comes easily to you.

Look out for physical feelings of heaviness and sluggishness. Try adding exercise to your routine and spices to your food (to improve digestion), and avoid heavy, slow-cooked foods, sugary snacks and dairy.

Not enough Earth in your chart

If you're low on Earth, you could lack understanding of the practical side of life – particularly how to make and respect both the material world and money. Your body and cycles will be out of tune with the present moment. You might lose traction and become disorganised, non-committal and lack awareness of what's going on around you.

A lack of Earth also results in an inner sense of insecurity, so you might find yourself overly concerned with money-making or buying property in order to find a material sense of security.

In terms of diet, heavy, warming foods that are high in nutrition are helpful here – try root vegetables and lots of protein to help balance out a deficiency of Earth.

If you lack Earth in your chart, import it! Invite Earth types into your life to teach you how to tap into your senses and feel present and grounded.

Air
Thinking

Gemini · Libra · Aquarius

Objective · Rational · Theoretical
Ideas-driven · Communicative

Air types understand the world through thought, ideas and communication. They need separation and space – they are able to remain individuals, rather than losing their sense of self by merging with another.

Air is the psychological opposite to Water, which means Air types are the least in touch with their feelings. They access their emotions via talking and sharing with others, employing intellectual introspection rather than simply sitting with their feelings. Feelings threaten their critical function of detachment and objectivity, as they endeavour to maintain a rational, open, non-judgmental and fair perspective rather than basing decisions on irrational feelings. Water types could find this attitude hard to live with.

Air types are curious. They have a bright mind and seek to connect both ideas and people. They are talkers who like to be involved in different topics of conversation.

They love spaciousness, not only in their mind and concepts, but in their environment. They prefer well-lit spaces, clean lines, panoramic views and open windows. They need plenty of stimulation as well as room to move around.

Too much Air in your chart

A lot of Air means a lot of talk! And a very busy mind. It means too much going on in your head and the world of ideas – you need to ground yourself into your body and the present.

You may put too much space between yourself and others in order to separate, which could mean finding yourself alone and lonely. You may need to learn how to take space rather than push others away to claim it. If given room to breathe, you won't feel the need to run away to get it.

Extremely detached, you may deflect a conversation or question if feelings are stirred, making it more impersonal and protecting yourself from difficult emotions. By disagreeing with others you maintain your sense of self.

Physically, skin and hair can be dry, and nails brittle. Air is light, dry and cold, so stay balanced by keeping warm, soaking up sunlight and avoiding wind. Eat warm, hearty, grounding meals. Hydrate with water and nourish your skin.

Not enough Air in your chart

Air helps us work through ideas and concepts in our minds, so with little to no Air, you will find this a more demanding task. Without the objectivity Air brings, you may become too invested or close to a situation. Your ability to step back and reflect may be hampered, and you might find yourself embroiled in conflict and challenging emotions, you may struggle to embrace new ideas and perhaps new people. Watch for getting stuck in your mindset.

Lack of Air is often compensated for by pursuing that element through further education, writing and perhaps excess communication in a bid to find clarity. Writing your thoughts out so that you can clearly see them and your options on paper is a great strategy. Journalling will change your life.

Add airy foods to your diet by eating grains, raw salads, light, dry foods like crackers, and cool, refreshing drinks.

If you lack Air in your chart, import it! Invite Air types into your life to teach you how to find perspective and separate thought from emotion.

Water
Feeling

Cancer · Scorpio · Pisces

**Emotional · Psychic · Sensitive
Instinctual · Empathetic · Nurturing**

Water employs feelings when it comes to making sense of the world. Their realm of perception is psychic. Highly attuned to the nuance and complexity of others, Water types pick up on seemingly hidden aspects of meaning. They have an ability to feel and connect emotionally with others, and their compassion and empathy are well developed. They seek to close the space between themselves and others, to merge.

Water is the least judgmental element – Water types just tune in and feel. Their vibe is usually a calming energy of acceptance and tolerance. They are the ultimate shapeshifter due to their changeability: they can be anything to anyone.

They remember experiences through feelings, learning best in an environment of love and support. If learning in a fearful environment they will pick things up, but can only reconnect back to the information through fear.

A tendency to yield can be seen as a weakness in our society. However, Water types win just by their ability to keep on hanging on. This is part of their great strength.

Air is psychologically the most different to Water. Air separates, just as the thought process separates from emotions. Water types can often attract Air types to help bring perspective, objectivity and a different way of understanding the world.

Too much Water in your chart

Like a psychic sponge, you're super-sensitive – you feel everything. Highly subjective, you may be out of touch with reality, in which case those feelings are even more amplified. Lots of tears are natural to you, as is a lot of love. You connect deeply and find it almost impossible to let go of anyone you've ever truly loved. Love can be unconditional, while sad times are felt exquisitely.

Where do you end and others begin? With little to no boundaries, you need a container of some sort. Earth can assist in defining a boundary for you, while Fire helps in terms of spiritual awareness. An artistic pursuit is ideal, as Water rules our imagination.

The changeable, flowing nature of Water means it's hard to stick on the same path. The most creative with the truth, Water can see you change your story to suit each listener.

You're drawn to living by water, which can help soothe the soul and revive after the drain of dealing with others and the realities of everyday life.

Melancholy can set in, so lean on Fire types to help brighten your mood and get plenty of natural light. Tough exercise is Fire-building, so get out and work up a sweat to beat the blues.

Not enough Water in your chart

Without enough Water, you'll feel out of touch with your own emotions. This could see you overcompensating by squeezing every drop of drama or emotion out of any given moment or situation. Instead, try to refine your emotional intelligence by seeking therapy or exercise that helps to put you in touch with yourself.

Hydration can be an issue, as can flushing toxins from your body, so be conscious about drinking enough water. Eat juicy fruits and vegetables.

If you lack Water in your chart, import it! Invite Water types into your life to teach you how to tap into your imagination, instinct and emotions.

Modes
Various vibrations

Also known as a 'quality' or 'modality', a mode describes the basic energetic approach of a sign. Each mode represents a different style of expression.

To help you relate to the modes, think of them as a super-efficient team of three that has been asked to bring a project from zero to hero. One of them needs to be an initiator who instigates the project (Cardinal). One needs to keep the project on target through the long and boring bits (Fixed). And the other needs to be responsive and adapt and move with the changes (Mutable).

Cardinal signs are Aries, Capricorn, Libra and Cancer. Fixed signs are Leo, Taurus, Aquarius and Scorpio. Mutable signs are Sagittarius, Virgo, Gemini and Pisces.

Each birth chart will have a different balance of modes. In some birth charts, the planets are evenly spread among the signs (and therefore modes), other birth charts see planets concentrated within certain signs and therefore potentially very low or high in one mode. As always, look at where the planets are positioned in your birth chart and see which signs (and modes) they fall into. Start with the personal planets and move on to the outer planets.

When a mode is missing or very low in a chart, it's useful to identify the missing mode's qualities in others, and work with those people for balance. If you are very high in one mode, see it as a super power and play to its strength.

Cardinal
Initiator

Aries · Cancer · Libra · Capricorn

Direct · Purposeful
Enterprising · Active

Cardinal gets the party started!

High in Cardinal

You're a born entrepreneur, someone who can't help but initiate. Full of get-up-and-go, you're a starter and doer. However, you may not be so great at maintaining energy for the long-haul and you're usually moving on to the next thing before finishing the first. Bear in mind, you'll need to work with others to bring a project to completion, and be mindful of burn-out – take breaks between projects or your health will suffer.

Low in Cardinal

Starting and initiating is not your strength, so work with someone who can help you to get projects and ideas off the ground. A coach could be useful in terms of rallying and cheerleading, especially if you have an idea or want to embark on a new path but are struggling to get going.

Fixed
Staying power

Taurus · Leo · Scorpio · Aquarius

Stable · Persistent · Constant
Determined · Persevering

Fixed holds the course steady!

High in fixed

You have a strong sense of self and can be a rock to others. Your loyalty is impressive. You can endure long hours at work and take projects through to completion. You need consistency and like to know the plan. Letting go is your Achilles heel, as you find change incredibly challenging.

Low in fixed

Staying on course is not your bag, so import some help if you need to see a project through – do this by hiring or working with a Fixed type.

Mutable
Versatile

Gemini · Virgo · Sagittarius · Pisces

Adaptable · Changeable · Versatile
Easily swayed · Multi-tasking

Mutable modifies and rolls with the changes!

High in Mutable

Highly adaptable, you can see myriad ways of approaching or completing a project and you work well with others. You can roll with change and follow new directions immediately. In fact, your impulse is to change direction and you need variety and stimulation in life. Be wary of feeling compelled to initiate change for the sake of it.

An overload of Mutable signs in your birth chart can mean you lose your sense of self or direction, becoming railroaded or overwhelmed by others' plans. Hire a coach or project manager to keep you on track. And seek out a Cardinal initiator to get your ideas off the ground, as well as a strong Fixed type to help you see your ideas through to completion.

You need frequent rest and routine can be difficult for you to establish, yet imperative in your life.

Low in Mutable

You struggle to adapt and change. You tend to be stable and know what you like and want. You hold a strong position or opinion and are not easily swayed by external conditions or opinions. Cultivate the art of compromise and co-operation, rather than forcing others to bend to your will.

IV. Houses

A birth chart is divided into 12 segments called houses. Each represents specific areas of life such as health and career. They are 'where' a function is being expressed. Remember, planets are 'what' is being expressed, and signs represent 'how' that function is being expressed. Houses are like the stage for a planet's expression. As with the planets and signs, use the keywords as a shorthand to their meaning.

Unlike signs, which each occupy 30° of the 360° birth chart, houses can occupy a bigger or smaller portion – these will vary from birth chart to birth chart. The beginning of each house is called the cusp, which will be at a specific degree to a sign (you will see the degree numbers when you create a birth chart). The sign on the cusp of each house (the smallest degree apart) is known as the ruling sign. The ruling sign flavours the affairs that house represents. For instance, if Libra is ruling the 6th House of mind/body, the flavour for that area of life would be Libran – therefore, you would express Libran traits of balance and harmony to sustain your physical and mental health.

If you can't identify the sign on the cusp of a house, you may have an 'intercepted' chart. This means you have a sign that begins and ends within a house (so the sign is engulfed by the house), and it therefore does not contain a cusp. In this case, there will be one sign ruling two house cusps elsewhere in the chart. The signs 'engulfed' in a house with no cusp to rule will be harder to express, and you will need conscious effort to do so. The same goes for the planets in those signs – you will have to employ conscious effort to express their function.

1st House
Ascendant

Rising sign · Self · Outlook
Appearance · First impressions
Personality · Vitality

ASSOCIATED with Aries, Mars
and Fire
POLARITY me vs we (1st vs 7th)

The cusp of the 1st House marks the position of your rising sign (also known as the ascendant sign). This sign, together with your Sun sign and Moon sign, should be read as one of the top three components of your chart: yes, it's really that informative!

The 1st House is important because it informs your outlook on life and your own concept of who you are. It tells you about you – from your personality and the way you express yourself, to the way you look and dress. The 1st House describes how we face new situations, experiences and the world in general. It's a Fire house, so it also gives you clues about your vitality, health and ability to assert yourself in the world.

The sign and planets in the 1st House inform the way you respond to new people and situations, and your initial boundaries.

Signs on the cusp of the 1st House (rising sign)

The rising sign is the outer image you present to the world – like your window dressing. People can take this at face value, or dig deeper to know you better. And often you will show people your 'front' first, and then reveal more about yourself (your Sun sign) when you feel more comfortable.

For example, if you have a reserved rising sign like Taurus, yet your Sun in feisty Leo, you'll start off slowly, then as friends get to know you, out comes the diva! The same is true in reverse. Imagine a party or unfamiliar situation. As a Leo rising you will launch yourself into the centre of the room, but if your Sun is in shy Pisces, you'll feel like a deer in the headlights and want to sidle off to the sidelines.

When feeling ratty, it's common to fall back on the traits of the rising sign and hide behind them. For example, Aries rising will turn on the assertion and start barking out commands. Taurus rising will head for quiet time and food.

Planets in the 1ˢᵗ House

Planets in the 1ˢᵗ House will be activated in new situations, and you'll seek new situations in which to access them. You'll find 1ˢᵗ House planets are particularly prominent and easily expressed. For example:

Venus · Adds charm and beauty – and you can be seen as being beautiful and charming.

Saturn · Adds maturity, reserve and a responsible outlook on life – you will keep your commitments! But you can be backward in coming forward in new situations and won't let many people through the front door on first contact.

Neptune · Lets anyone in, no restrictions. It lends an openness to new encounters.

A focus on the 1ˢᵗ House in your chart

A lot of planets in the 1ˢᵗ House suggest you will be up front initially and can make an impression. You'll have quite a strong sense of 'I am' and will be subjective. You'll learn a lot about yourself from how the world responds to you in initial interactions.

2nd House

Self worth · Values · Resources
Money · Income · Material
possessions · Abundance

ASSOCIATED with Taurus, Venus and Earth
POLARITY mine vs yours/ours (2nd vs 8th)

The 2nd House is all about the self-worth that underpins external wealth. As an Earth house it's also associated with building foundations. And through its correspondence with Taurus, this house cements its theme of being about acquisition, your relationship with money and with your own body. How do you look after yourself? What do you spend your money on? It's all about: 'what is mine; what am I doing with it?'

Our own values and self-worth are intricately connected with what we believe we deserve and indeed are even capable of achieving. The power of manifesting is key here. For example, if you need to clear some money blocks, check out what's going on in the 2nd House. But remember the key to abundance (and manifesting) is to see evidence of what you want already existing in your world. In other words, come from a place of already having it, and trusting there's enough in the world, rather than a place of lack or 'I should have/I want'. Manifesting is much more effective when you start from a belief in the abundance of what you already have.

Your outcome will always be congruent with your inner story. Material wealth will level out to what you believe you're worth, so change your story to change your world.

Signs on the cusp of the 2nd House

The 2nd House indicates the talent you're paid for, so focus on it in interviews and career choices. The sign on the cusp reveals the nature of your value system and natural talents. For example, if you have Gemini on the cusp, it will indicate your ability and your interest in connecting people, communications and writing. These will be highly prized personal resources. Communications are the key to your income so hone that skill.

Planets in the 2nd House

Planets positioned in the 2nd House indicate an area of self worth. By actively expressing them, they will be key to building your material foundations. For example:

Sun · You will benefit from that star's creative expression. If you have this placement, you may also identify with your 'things'. Remember this: 'My worth is what I have,' so you'll place value on possessions, and what you spend your money on. They'll have to reflect your sterling idea of self. But – build up an inner sense of worth rather than leaning on material possessions to let the world know how fabulous you are.

Mars · You have drive and energy to burn in terms of making money and physical challenges. You place value on your energy and the ability to act on your own terms, so think about how you are utilising your entrepreneurial skills and your energy. How are you actively building your resources?

Uranus · You will have unusual values, or those values may be about change. You'll be prone to giving away possessions, or suddenly losing or acquiring them.

A focus on the 2nd House in your chart

If you have several planets in the 2nd House, 'I'm worth it' is your mantra, so aim high. A lot of planets in the 2nd House also means you have a variety of resources to draw from and always have what you need. You'll learn about yourself through how you make money. Your dream may be centred around creating or building something material. A straw bale house, a tarot deck, beautiful furniture or a healthy investment portfolio – doesn't matter! You enjoy the physical comforts of life and delight in your material possessions.

3rd House

Rational mind · Facts · Learning
Relationships based on proximity
Local environment

ASSOCIATED with Gemini, Mercury and Air

POLARITY facts vs meaning (3rd vs 9th)

The 3rd House is the first of the Air houses, which gives it a focus on communications. Relationships that are based on proximity come under this house, be it with siblings, neighbours or the even the local barista.

There's also an emphasis on education and learning. There are various levels of the mind and the 3rd House represents the factual, rational level: basic learning. It covers the kind of environment you need to be in in order to best learn. How do you process that learning? And how do you share it? These questions are answered by the 3rd House.

Another area of life represented by the 3rd House is our local environment and how we respond to social connections within it. The kind of environment we need to feel connected socially will be decided by the sign on the cusp.

Signs on the cusp of the 3rd House

The sign on the cusp will indicate your preferred learning style. For example, Cancer on the cusp you'll need to feel emotionally safe and cared for in order to learn. Any threat to that comfort will shut your mind down until you feel safe again – you excel when teachers mother you! Aries on the cusp? You will learn quickly and be keen to pick up new things. If you are a Fire sign, you'll constantly be looking for stimulation, otherwise you become bored and distracted. And if you are an Earth sign, you might learn well kinesthetically, especially if given a practical reason for learning.

Planets in the 3rd House

Planets located in the 3rd House will express through communication, education/learning and connections in the local environment. For example:

Sun · You will shine in your local area and be fairly well known: you'll want the local baker and banker to know you by name. Your ability to communicate and network helps define your sense of self.

Venus · You enjoy pleasant relationships with locals and neighbours, as well as with brothers and sisters. You'll find pleasure and value in learning.

Mercury · You'll be curious about what's happening locally, have talent in writing and communications, and enjoy learning facts and details.

A focus on the 3rd House in your chart

With a lot of planets in the 3rd House, you'll place importance on sibling relationships, perhaps being influenced by them. The local community will be important and you may contribute by being involved. Continuing to build knowledge will be important, and you may learn by simply exchanging ideas. Keeping up with local news and social connections will be vital.

Since the local environment is ruled by the 3rd House, short-distance travel is also a feature in your life, along with the modes of transport involved. You'll be busy getting out and about and forming connections.

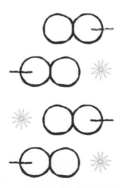

4th House

Home · Family roots · Belonging
Real estate · Private self
Emotional underpinnings

ASSOCIATED with Cancer, Moon and Water
POLARITY private home vs public world (4th vs 10th)

The 4th House describes your home base in all of its shapes – from the physical structure of a home to a sense of belonging and feeling grounded. It's also associated with family roots, emotional heritage and also real estate.

As a Water house, the 4th represents your psychological make-up and often reveals either hidden treasure or complexes that might have left you troubled. Therapies that explore the past and emotional life are worthwhile for any one who has a difficult aspect in their chart in this area.

Our sense of emotional attachment and of feeling rooted are informed by our family background, so your connection between home and inner security can be found here in the 4th House.

Signs on the cusp of the 4th House

The sign on the cusp will indicate your style of home-making. For example, Cancer will go for creature comforts and a family-home vibe. Whereas Sagittarius will be active in the house – maybe you have a home gym, tennis court or running track, or would at least appreciate those things!

Planets in the 4th House

Planets in the 4th House will indicate what part of yourself you express at home. For example:
Uranus · You may experience a desire for sudden change (in location or look), or even unorthodox ways of decorating, or

Uranus · You may experience a desire for sudden change (in location or look), or even unorthodox ways of decorating, or living communally. Tech could be a feature of the home.

Jupiter · You love a large home for entertaining. A base of faith and abundance is the bedrock of your inner foundations, while being at home is where you tap into inspiration. There will be good relationships with flatmates and family, of which there may be many.

Chiron · This planet suggests you have a wounding related to the home or family. You may have been fostered or taken in by others, or feel abandoned in some way. You may turn your home into a place of healing for others who you sense need care or support.

A focus on the 4ᵗʰ House in your chart

We all need a secure place to call home where we can relax, recharge and let go of the outside world for a while. If your 4ᵗʰ House is packed with planets, this is even more vital. You'll have quite the homebody side and family is your rock. Checking in will be important regardless of what else is going on in the world. Take time to explore your internal emotions, and leave time to rest and digest your experience.

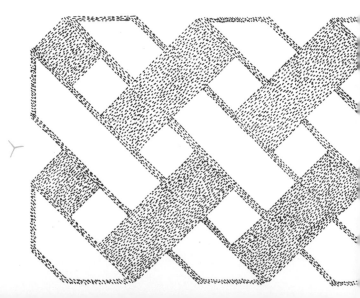

Star Power

5th House

Romance · Creative self-expression
Fun/pastimes · Children · Inner child
Speculation · Fame

ASSOCIATED with Leo, Sun and Fire
POLARITY personal expression vs group
contribution (5th vs 11th)

The 5th House is the area of our life where you create for pure joy and pleasure rather than for an outcome of money or for service.

The second of the Fire houses, the 5th is all about our flame of self-expression and it represents our creative outlets. This is also where you will encourage your inner child to play and frolic. We all need joy in life, and to feel free to express ourselves – it's essential in order to remain vital – and one way of nurturing more of that is to see things from the perspective of your four- or five-year-old self: this was a time when you didn't identify with your job or 'status'. Take time to operate from this perspective and hug your inner child!

Children are a feature of the 5th, since unless you are an artist, child-bearing is the most creative act you will achieve – they essentially connect you back to your own inner child and the joy of open-hearted expression.

Since this is our house of play, it concerns what we do to entertain ourselves, our own ability to entertain and what kind of entertainment we enjoy.

Signs on the cusp of the 5th House

The sign on the cusp will indicate your style of play-making, your sense of fun and approach to the pleasure that is romance. For example, Aries will be keen on action adventure and sports activities, and a leader in initiating fun or romance. Virgo will go about organising fun events and find joy in health-oriented activities. Nutrition is her idea of fun. Dating will be by the rule book and she'll appreciate doing things the old-fashioned way.

Capricorn will be an authority in some capacity… captain of the sports team? Romance will be taken seriously, dutifully and traditionally.

Planets in the 5th House

Planets located in the 5th house express through creativity, romance and pleasure. For example:

Pluto · You'll seek transformation through your creativity; in romance you'll want intensity, passion and a key to your love's heart. You might have a penchant for psychological thrillers.

Uranus · Sci-fi will be high on the movie list. Love will hit you like a lightning bolt – and sometimes end just as abruptly.

Jupiter · You'll be multi-talented, full of self-belief in your creative output, generous creatively and lucky in romance!

A focus on the 5th House in your chart

If you have lots of planets in the 5th House, you will need arts in your life and romance will be vital throughout life. Children will feature: you may have your own children or work with them in some capacity – either way, they will bring you great joy. The Sun in the 5th will be glamorous – you will shine in these areas and you'll need to play in order to connect with yourself and build your identity. Let your inner celebrity shine: you were meant to be famous. In romance you'll enjoy creative types.

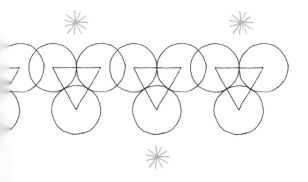

6th House

Health · Mind-body connection
Daily routine · Daily work
Service · Pets

ASSOCIATED with Virgo, Mercury
and Earth
POLARITY grounding routine
vs timeless transcendence (6th vs 12th)

The 6th House is associated with your daily routine and your approach to work, as well as the environment you work in.

It also indicates your health, particularly your mind-body connection. As we all know, our mind and body are intimately linked. When our thoughts or actions are out of alignment with our values, needs and authenticity, it can manifest in physical responses and ailments. Our mind affects our body's chemistry, while our body's messages to our mind can also alter its state. This feedback loop can rule us, or we can take the driver's seat and maintain a healthy routine, diet and exercise to keep our systems purring.

Pets and plants come under the 6th House domain, as they act as anchors requiring a care routine, calling you home to touch base daily. Returning home is part of a healthy daily routine – without this, you could end up running from one thing to the next and end up feeling ragged, drained or unbalanced.

Signs on the cusp of the 6th House

Since health is an area ruled by the 6th, the sign on the cusp tells us what we need daily to keep us feeling well and balanced. For example, Libra needs to connect socially, works well in a dynamic duo and needs harmony in order to thrive.

The sign on the cusp also infers the type of personal imbalance that will let you know when things are getting out of sync. Bring in more traits of this sign if you're feeling off kilter. Look at the Signs chapter (see page 70) to identify the body parts ruled by each sign – this will be the area where problems show up physically. For example, Taurus will experience neck and throat issues when being harried or bullied: stiffness in general can be a problem.

Planets in the 6th House

Planets in the 6th House indicate what part of you needs expression in your daily routine and work environment, as well as health. For example:

Moon · You may work with women, connect emotionally to your workplace, seek emotional connection in general and find yourself in a nurturing role. You may be a mother figure in the office. Disruption at work tends to affect you emotionally.

Pluto · You will need depth and challenge in the workplace. If you start to feel that you need transformation at work and a change of scene or challenge, you'll find that your body will rebel if you don't do something about it. You have a strong regenerative capacity to your health. You could have a capacity for energy healing.

A focus on the 6th House in your chart

If you have a lot of planets in the 6th, you could tend towards workaholism. However, your body will let you know when you're overdoing it – it's like a canary in the coal mine to ensure you maintain a work/life balance and love what you do, so listen to it! A focus in the 6th will also bring an understanding of, and interest in, natural holistic healing. Your body will react quickly to imbalance, but can restore itself quickly too – if you take the right measures.

You learn almost by osmosis, so surround yourself with the best when you want to pick up new skills. You're built for service and find great satisfaction in (fulfilling) work – a nurturing work environment is vital to your wellbeing. In ancient times, this house was called the 'house of slavery'. Thankfully for 6th House people, times have changed!

7ᵗʰ **House**
Descendent

Equal partnership · Marriage
Contracts · Counselling
Projection · Rivals

ASSOCIATED with Libra, Venus and Air
POLARITY we vs me (7ᵗʰ vs 1ˢᵗ)

This is the relationship house. All significant partnerships are indicated, the key being that they're equal in nature – so it could be a romantic partnership, a business one or anything inbetween. The cusp sign and planets found in this house describe our partnerships, what we look for in a partner, what we bring to a partnership, and what kind of partnership we want. Contractual agreements of all types fall under 7ᵗʰ House rule, including marriage.

Second of the Air houses, the 7ᵗʰ is social, and all about one-to-one contact with another: often a significant other. Since it's opposite, the 1ˢᵗ House of me, me, me, the 7ᵗʰ is in polarity, calling you, you, you. So while the 5ᵗʰ House rules romance and love affairs, when these relationships evolve to the next level, it's the 7ᵗʰ House you need to look to.

Perhaps most importantly, this is an area in which we project part of ourselves onto others like a mirror. They can reflect our own unacknowledged, unclaimed or repressed traits – ideally we can claim them back and integrate them. Relationship patterns that seem to repeat can often be traced back to the planets or sign of this house.

Signs on the cusp of the 7ᵗʰ House

Signs on the cusp will reflect the type of partnerships you make and the approach you take. For example, Aries on the cusp is assertive, needs 'me' time and is very direct. While Scorpio will demand a certain depth, loyalty and passion. Gemini may be able to sustain more than one partnership, while preferring to keep it light and breezy.

The sign on the cusp of the 7th House is also the descendent, and can indicate the traits projected onto others, when you don't own them in yourself. For example, Scorpio descendent needs to accept they are intense in love. Gemini, own that fickle side, accept that you need multiple stimulation and that it's OK not to get everything from one person.

Until those traits are owned, they are worn by people we're attracted to, eventually expressing the negative side of each sign or planet, in order to force us to own it in ourselves.

Planets in the 7th House

Planets located in the 7th House describe what part of yourself you express in relationships. For example:

Sun · You shine here, bringing a conscious approach to relationships, as well as great skill in creating harmony and in negotiating. In projection, the Sun becomes the big personality you're attracted to, who then devolves into overbearing and annoying. You need to own your shine. Claim it, don't project it!

Venus · You love to love. You connect through your charm and diplomacy, with everyone from the grocer to your lover. In projection, you become co-dependent. Instead, take back your ability to love everyone you meet.

Uranus · You experience sudden beginnings and endings, a need for autonomy and perhaps an unusual match or living arrangement.

A focus on the 7th House in your chart

Relationships will be a focal point for those with lots of planets in the 7th House, especially with Sun, Moon or Venus in this house. This is the area of life where you'll achieve the most self-development. Front-of-house jobs or public relations positions are great for this placement, plus any kind of counselling role. Founders of modern psychology, Carl Jung and Sigmund Freud, both had Sun in the 7th, as well as other planets.

8th House

Other people's resources · Sex
Death · Metaphysical · Psychic
development · Afterlife

ASSOCIATED with Scorpio, Pluto and
Water
POLARITY: ours vs mine (8th vs 2nd)

The 8th House is the area of life in which we merge our resources deeply with others. It's about the wealth of that partnership, about joining assets, and how to get the most out of coming together with someone else. It also indicates the resources of others we can access, which could be emotional, financial, or anything inbetween.

In the divorce courts, this is where you find yourself. Will you let it transform you or will you go down in flames? Want to know who you're really getting into bed with? Look no further than the 8th House.

Incidentally, this is also the house of sex, because it's an area in which you merge deeply with another, for a short time transcending ego in union. Tantric sex is on the radar too, and falls into this house as a great example of how to work spiritually by combining your energetic and physical resource (your body) with another's to transcend and transform. The power of sexuality is found, explored and expressed here.

Signs on the cusp of the 8th House

The sign on the 8th House cusp describes your approach to all things hidden, shared and sex. For example, Aries will charge in where angels fear to tread. Sexually, you'll like conquest. Sagittarius, you will want to explore and find meaning. Sexually, you'll be athletic! Pisces may lack boundaries and be aware of subtle paranormal activity. If you believe, then ghosts come under the 8th as they are beyond the physical realm and exist in the psychic/metaphysical.

Planets in the 8th House

Planets located in the 8th House will need expression as a shared resource or reflect parts of you that are operating on a deep and hidden level. For example:

Venus · You'll lean towards dark, moody and artistically broody. Love will need to be transformative, deep and loyal. This is an excellent placement in terms of other people's money! Money may be made from taboo, divinatory or metaphysical arts like astrology.

Neptune · You will be loose with boundaries when it comes to sex. Sex can be a truly blissful and transcendental union, so choose your lover wisely to make the most of this one.

Moon · You can psychically pick up on all the unsaid emotional vibes in the room.

Sun · The Sun here has an intense will. You will shine when combining talents and undergo cycles of serious personal transformation and growth.

Uranus · You'll experience sudden windfalls, endings and beginnings. You have an ability to make use of others' unique genius... and an experimental or freaky side in the bedroom! You'll be totally up for trying new things.

A focus on the 8th House in your chart

Have lots of planets in the 8th House? If it's taboo, a mystery or in any way obscured, you will find it. What's under that? What's in there? You need to know what's hidden and you'll ferret out any private, secret business. There will be a psychic and metaphysical channel of understanding, and a cyclical urge to create endings in order to transform and grow, like the way a snake sheds its skin. You work well with others' resources – you'd make a great investment banker. You're not interested in superficial small talk, but there's a magnetic intensity and a focused will.

9th House

Higher mind · Higher education
Philosophy · International travel
Publishing · Religion

ASSOCIATED with Sagittarius, Jupiter and Fire
POLARITY higher meaning vs logical facts (9th vs 3rd)

Opposite the 3rd House of facts, logical communication and local interactions, the 9th represents the seeker, the lifelong student and the teacher. This is where we cultivate our higher mind, search for and make meaning out of facts, and develop our beliefs, ethics and personal philosophies. The light of inspiration burns bright here and beckons us to pursue it.

This house rules anything that expands our understanding and broadens our mind. Higher education, international travel, exposure to foreign people and cultures – all extend our experience beyond the community we were raised in. A focus on higher consciousness and spiritual thought make this the house of organised religion.

If it's cross-cultural and involves crossing borders, it probably has correlations with the 9th House. International trade and large multinational corporations are represented in the 9th. Publishing falls under this house since it brings education and knowledge to the masses. Government and law is also associated, with ethics being a high priority of this area.

Signs on the cusp of the 9th House

The sign on the cusp of the 9th House describes your approach to anything that expands your experience and develops your personal philosophies. For example, Virgo will set the scene for a thoughtful, contemplative approach to philosophy and belief. Simple paths like Zen will appeal to you. Capricorn, you may cling to traditional beliefs and need proof before you change beliefs. In higher education, you'll want to go through established channels. Aquarius will be open minded and entertain unorthodox beliefs. Your philosophy will involve Aquarian traits of liberty, fraternity and have a humanitarian bent.

Planets in the 9th House

Planets located in the 9th House indicate a part of yourself seeking expansion beyond your personal borders, whether mental or physical. For example:

Sun · You will learn and develop by exposing yourself to foreign cultures, people, customs and ideas. A natural teacher, you like sharing all you learn.

Venus · You love travel for pleasure and have good experiences abroad.

Mars · You enjoy adventurous and intrepid travel. You also make a lively philosophical debator, and want to express your beliefs actively – and will be ready to fight for them. A martial art would suit you.

A focus on the 9th House in your chart

A lot of planets in the 9th House will indicate a restless spirit and a natural seeker – travel, foreign cultures and higher education will draw you in, and you'll have a natural tendency to teach. A strong philosophical approach to life will be apparent. Religious contemplation will be guaranteed, but a commitment won't need to be made to any one doctrine.

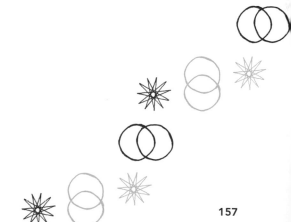

10th House

Career · Public Image · Reputation
Status · Public contribution · Goals
Ambition

ASSOCIATED with Capricorn, Saturn
and Earth
POLARITY public world vs private home
(10th vs 4th)

The 10th House is concerned with your contribution to the world at large. The 10th is your public image and social contribution. Your vocation is your calling to serve as well as how you want to be seen professionally, so this house will tell you a lot about your career. The image you deliberately cultivate to be seen by society is suggested here. And your responsibility to society, as well as to yourself, comes under this house.

The Medium Coeli – middle of the sky – is the topmost point of the Sun's daily journey, therefore it represents our highest goals and aspirations. Fame, or what you become known for, is indicated by this house since it's so public.

An inner sense of status is key to developing an external expression. Bosses and challenges in career present in this house, as well as our personal gifts and how we use them – whether to gratify ego and seek power, or for the greater good of society.

Signs on the cusp of the 10th House

The sign on the cusp of the 10th House indicates the nature and approach to your career and public image. For example, Aquarius will want to be seen as unusual, unique and individual. You'll do things differently and need that opposite 4th House with Leo on the cusp to provide the confidence to do that. You may be ahead of the curve, or work in science or advanced tech. Capricorn will prefer a traditional career and route – you'll be keen to work your way up and have your name on the door, if not run the country. Libra careers will involve a skill for negotiation, compromise, beauty or the arts. Interior design, fashion, style or even counselling are all career choices and images that suit.

Planets in the 10th House

Planets located in the 10th House need expression in your career and public life. And we are known by others (or the public realm) for the function of planets in the 10th. For example:

Mars · You will be active in career – it may literally be physically demanding or involve movement or leadership. You will be seen as energetic and possibly a leader.

Jupiter · You bring an approach of luck and faith to your career, taking big leaps and landing on your feet. You'll be seen as a generous, larger-than-life person bringing expansion and uplift as part of your role.

Moon · You seek emotional connection in your career. With a gut instinct for what the public wants, you may speak to a female demographic. Your career may involve sharing your emotional life and you'll appear as a soft and caring person.

A focus on the 10th House in your chart

With a lot of planets in the 10th House, you'll be ambitious and career-oriented, so a suitable career path that allows you to grow is vital. This is the arena in which you'll learn about and test your mettle in order to distinguish yourself. You'll want to develop systems and implement them. Often a gifted leader, you'll need autonomy. A steady path to the top will suit you, while recognition, status and potentially fame is on the cards, at least in your field. Feeling a sense of duty to the larger community, you will want to contribute something worthwhile. Do your best to take responsibility and move mountains. If you are a 10th House person, it's your duty to go for it with integrity and authority, setting the standard for others to follow.

11ᵗʰ House

Groups · Peers · Kindred spirits
Social ideals and activism · Altruism
Future vision

ASSOCIATED with Aquarius, Uranus and Air
POLARITY group contribution vs personal expression (11ᵗʰ vs 5ᵗʰ)

The 11ᵗʰ has a focus on broad social ideals. Groups fall under its domain, particularly peer groups. This is the tribe you run with, which reflects your social spirit. It's all about how you relate in and to larger groups rather than your individual, personal expression.

The 11ᵗʰ House describes your approach to humanitarian issues and what, if anything, you're motivated to do about them. How you maintain your identity within a group, as well as respond to it, is described by the sign on the cusp and any planets within the house.

If you build a community in connection with your profession, it's represented here. Friends and colleagues that are like-minded or share a particular common interest assure us we don't walk alone. Large group marches, uprisings and the power of the people to change society are all represented by the 11ᵗʰ House. This is an area of life where you reach out beyond your own personal interests to connect beyond ego, in order to bring about change. For this reason, the 11ᵗʰ is also concerned with future hopes, dreams and wishes.

Signs on the cusp of the 11ᵗʰ House

The sign on the cusp of the 11ᵗʰ House indicates your approach to groups, peers and wider societal concerns. For example, Capricorn will organise a group and happily take up responsible positions like sitting on committees. Authority in groups is key. Sagittarius will roam between diverse groups. You may be attracted to people from different cultures, groups founded on varying religious practice, or even sports groups.

Planets in the 11ᵗʰ House

Planets located in the 11ᵗʰ House need expression in groups and the wider social milieu. For example:

Moon · You seek nurture from groups, which often comprise women. You may love to eat out as well as nurture your friends. You will have a passion for social movements and trends. Humanitarian and social ideals centre around women's rights, and especially mothers.

Venus · You love being social and benefit from extending your network. Your ideals are formed around beauty, arts and relationships. Women's rights may also feature in your ideals and causes.

Chiron · You will have wounding around fitting in with peers or groups, therefore you have skills to heal or counter this issue in others. You may take others under your wing.

A focus on the 11ᵗʰ House in your chart

A socialite with the heart of an activist: you're all about the group and humanitarian ideals. With lots of planets in the 11ᵗʰ House, you'll be comfortable with an entourage, you thrive being out and about, and enjoy a wide circle of diverse friends. You find a platform of equality with everyone you meet, whether royalty or regular Joe, which is a great part of your charm and gifts. There may be a particular peer group you relate to for a common cause, while meeting random people from all walks of life encourages personal growth. You are a communal person and team player. When you align your social ideals with that of a group, everyone wins.

12th House

Transcendence · Collective
consciousness · Subconsciousness
Solitude · Personal Undoing

ASSOCIATED with Pisces, Neptune
and Water
POLARITY timeless transcendence vs
daily grounding measures (12th vs 6th)

The final house of the birth chart, the 12th House indicates how we retreat into our inner space and what parts of ourselves need expression here.

This house is pure mystic: nebulous, non-material and rather mysterious to Western culture. Eastern cultures have been mining its depths for thousands of years, actuating precise techniques and descriptions of how to access its gifts. When you meditate, dream, become lost to yourself, beyond your sense of self, you have entered this house. The 12th is truly the domain of your inner connection to the sublime, blissful, egoless state we call 'goddess'.

In ancient times, this house was referred to as the house of sickness, of hidden enemies, of self-undoing and of institutions that incarcerate, like asylums and hospitals. This is due to our own subconscious habits, patterns and hidden complexes that trip us up. Exploring the contents of our unconscious and making it conscious is the path to clearing blocks that hinder. The 6th House polarity suggests that it's the routine, groundedness and health of the body that allow us to enjoy the liberating aspect of the 12th. The work and service implied by the 6th House also suggest how important it is to respect and maintain this area of life in order to seek liberation. Without grounding suggested by the 6th House one may become unravelled, lost or out of touch with 'reality'.

Thankfully, our generation of modern mystics understands the value and necessity of exploring our interior selves and the hidden wealth to be found there, while balancing the great opportunities continually opening up in life, work and love.

Signs on the cusp of the 12ᵗʰ House

Signs on the cusp of the 12ᵗʰ House describe your approach to the subconscious, collective and transcendent zone. For example, Aries will have a fearless approach to the unknown. You want to challenge yourself to explore more, but your undoing will be a lack of patience, or an aggressive attitude. Taurus, you will find transcendence through communing in nature's temple. Music or getting lost in practical arts and crafts are also avenues for this sensual sign. Attachment to material possessions can stand in the way of liberation, as can pure stubbornness and inflexibility.

Planets in the 12ᵗʰ House

Planets in the 12ᵗʰ House indicate what part of you needs expression through solitary or transcendent pursuits. This part is in tune with the collective unconscious. For example:

Sun · You need time out to get back in touch with yourself. Highly impressionable, insights will be picked up by channelling the vibe around you. Your downfall is ego, so stay humble.

Uranus · You'll experience sudden insight from the unconscious and take an experimental approach to mystical pursuits.

Saturn · This could indicate fear around the unknown and letting go. Find a structured approach like guided visualisation. Controlling behaviour and fear are your undoing.

A focus on the 12ᵗʰ House in your chart

A lot of planets in the 12ᵗʰ House make you a natural Houdini, with an urge to escape from day-to-day mundane existence. Say 'no' to drugs, alcohol and other addictions that promise escape but threaten to wreck. Say 'yes' to meditation or forms of quiet contemplation. You need periods of solitude to centre and connect to yourself – to lose then find yourself. You could benefit from acting or any form of testing out different identities. Find ways of not being 'you' for a while. You have a soft, compassionate side with a desire to help the downtrodden. Channel your natural understanding into writing, teaching or art. Spiritual guidance could be an interesting path.

V. Aspects

Ever wondered what all of those little numbers mean on your birth chart? They indicate the relationship between planets and a sign, as well as house cusps and a sign. Alongside each planet, you will see a degree number between 0° and 29° – this indicates the degree it is located within a sign. Remember, each sign covers 30° of the chart.

You can also use these degrees to measure the degrees between two planets or points – and this is how you will know the type of aspect they form.

An aspect is a geometric angle between two points in the chart – for example, a square aspect is a 90° angle. The five major aspects are the conjunction, sextile, square, trine and opposition. There are other more minor aspects, but let's keep it simple and go for the big ticket items!

Because hitting a round number (such as an even 90°) is tricky, there is a tolerance of degree allowed, known as an 'orb'. This orb indicates the allowance of degrees an aspect can make and remain classed as that aspect.

The aspects formed by two or more planets act as conduits, either bringing the function of those planets together, or putting them into conflict. This harmony or conflict can be experienced emotionally, psychologically and even in the form of events. Learn to understand the different aspects and their impact in order to understand how the planets in your chart relate and affect each other.

♂
Conjunction
Merging functions

0° in the birth chart
Orb of 5° for the planets
Orb of 10° degrees for the Sun or Moon

Conjunct planets are two or more planets that are placed side by side each other in your birth chart. Their function is merged – whenever one planet is activated, so is the other. The closer they are in degrees, the more their energy is merged. This aspect can release variable sides of the planets and signs involved, not just the positive ones. Work consciously with it to ensure you get the best out of both planets.

Planets conjunct in a birth chart

Venus conjunct Mercury · Venus (love, relating) will lend its beauty and charm to Mercury's function of communication. The result is you will be a delightful speaker, have a pleasant voice and be creative in your expression through speech and writing. You love listening, learning and talking, and the way to your heart is through the literal language of love. You'll be interested in and think about love, relationships and beauty. There will be clever ideas around how to make money as well as judgements on what things are worth, including people!

Sun conjuct Mars · Any planet conjuct the Sun will have an impact and be an obvious part of your personality. In this case, Mars (strong, assertive) conjunct the Sun (self, power) might mean you doesn't see how aggressive or dominating you can be. You'll easily assert your will and personal needs.

Moon conjuct Nepture · Your Moon (emotion) conjunct Neptune (sensitivity, imagination) could mean an extremely sensitive and emotional nature. You might be compassionate as well as intuitive, and there might be a natural mystic or artist within.

Look out for a stellium

Three or more planets bunched up together (connected by conjunctions) is called a stellium. If you have this in your birth chart, think of it like wild stallions running together: in combination, they're a force of nature and can plough through anything they encounter. The sign and house a stellium is found in will indicate the direction the planets in the stellium will aim towards.

For example, a stellium of planets in the 10th House (career, social status) will indicate that career and public image is the focal point. Your energy will consistently need expression in your work, and without sufficient outlet for this energy, you will never meet your potential. You need to find a peak you want to climb and climb it.

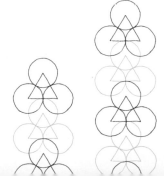

✳

Sextile
Opportunities

60° degrees apart in the birth chart
Orb of 4° for the planets
Orb of 8° for the Sun or Moon

As the name suggests this is rather a pleasant and easy aspect that needs only a slight effort to activate. It's harmonious, therefore the positive influence of both planets are released. It suggests a person will have natural gifts connected to the planets in this aspect. Check your chart for sextiles so you can be aware of and celebrate your strengths.

Planets in sextile in a birth chart

Sun in sextile with Pluto · The 60° separation between Sun (self) and Pluto (insight, transformation) suggests an ability to regenerate yourself, as well as transform your identity with ease. You have access to a natural magnetism and personal power when you need it rather than it being 'on' all the time, as you might find if these planets were in conjunction or trine.

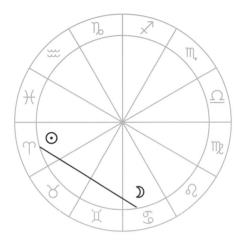

□
Square
*Dynamic &
challenging*

90° apart in the birth chart
Orb of 5° for planets
Orb of 10° for the Sun or Moon

This is the most challenging aspect planets can form. It suggests each planet and its function is completely at odds with the other. If you have this aspect in your chart, you'll need to apply a lot of awareness and conscious effort to make the most of the tension involved. This is also the most dynamic aspect, with a lot of potential if you're willing to do the work. The square forces change, it's constant and compelling. Think of it as the grit that makes the pearl. Internally it can manifest as a tension that, at its best, results in drive. Externally it can manifest in two conflicting areas of life that don't seem to work together well.

Four planets 90° away from each other around a birth chart form a 'grand square'. This aspect pattern is extremely tense and challenging. The planets, houses and signs involved need to be considered and conflicts addressed, or they will work against each other. There is great drive here for evolution, however it will only come with awareness and self-growth.

Planets in square in a birth chart

These planets are at cross purposes and there may well be a power struggle. The problem is that one planet will always be dominating the other. Usually the outer planet projects negative traits on the inner planet. For example:

Uranus in square with the Sun · Outer planet Uranus (change) conflicting with inner planet Sun (self) could mean self expression is volatile and erratic. The rebelliousness of Uranus is overdone and doesn't support a sense of self. Learn to channel the eccentricity of Uranus to create unique self-expression.

Planets in square – look at houses

If you have a square aspect, identify which houses the planets in this square fall into. These are the areas that will seem at odds with each other in your life. For example, if one planet is in the 10th House of career and the other is in the 7th of partnerships, the square will create tension and challenge in these two areas of life. Perhaps you have to travel for work, causing a knock on effect and problems with your partner. To address this, you'll need to address your inner conflict and then also compromise externally. You could find a career where you can work with your partner, which could be incredibly dynamic, yet require effort to maintain.

Planets in square – look at signs

If you have a square aspect, identify which signs the planets in this square fall into. Are the signs compatible with each other? What do the planets bring to the signs? For example, if the square sees the Sun (self) fall in Sagittarius (visionary), and Mars (action) fall in Virgo (detail), it could be a volatile square. You'll need to think about how to find some common ground between these two signs, or a way they can contribute to each other. Sagittarius is interested in the bigger picture, while Virgo is all about detail. It will take self-reflection and discipline to bring this square together harmoniously.

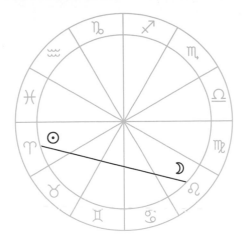

△
Trine
Harmonious

120° apart in the birth chart
Orb of 5° for planets
Orb of 10° for the Sun or Moon

Everyone wants the trines! Planets in trine with each other work in harmony. There is complete ease and no effort needed to get the most out of the connection. If there are difficult aspects in the chart, the trines are a place to lean into when times are tough. These are your strengths, so get to know them!

Like all things, even easy street has a dark side. Too many trines can indicate laziness and an expectation that everything will come with no effort, because it usually does. There's no tension compelling you to work hard to achieve your dreams. Make sure you don't get complacent!

Planets in trine in your birth chart

Planets in trine will share the same element. If you find that you have three planets in trine, each 120° apart, and each sharing an element, you have what's known as a 'grande trine'. This is a particularly easy expression of the planets – no effort needed.

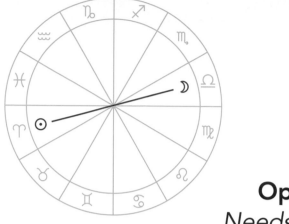

Opposition
Needs balance

180° apart in the birth chart
Orb of 5° for planets
Orb of 10° for the Sun or Moon

The opposition of planets requires balance. It suggests the polar ends of two spectrums by sign and house. Finding the neutral point where these spectrums merge is a key.

There is a tendency to identify with an inner planet, leaving the function of the outer planet in opposition ignored, because it might be too powerful to accept. Sometimes we swing back and forth between the two functions of those planets. The best approach is to focus on and give each planet equal amounts of time and attention (in terms of how the planet's function manifests in your nature). This will help you integrate the polarities in your nature.

Planets in opposition in a birth chart

Let's look at an example: the Moon (emotions) in the 11th House (groups, social ideas) is in opposition to Venus (love, relating) in the 5th House (romance, creativity).

You prefer to be in a group and enjoy sharing emotions. You take an interest in other people's emotions. You want to express your feelings for social change on issues like women's rights or motherhood. But Venus in 5th indicates you need time out to pursue your own personal brand of creative self-expression and have one-on-one time in love affairs that light you up and inspire you. If either the Moon or Venus are ignored – and you give all your energy and attention to either emotions or love – you might end up missing out on one or the other.

Alternatively, you can look at an opposition as two parts of a person's nature. You might feel you only have access to one function at a time. You may have difficulty feeling (Moon) loved (Venus) – because the Moon and Venus are in opposition. Awareness means we can apply ourselves to self-growth and learn how to bring these two parts of our nature together.

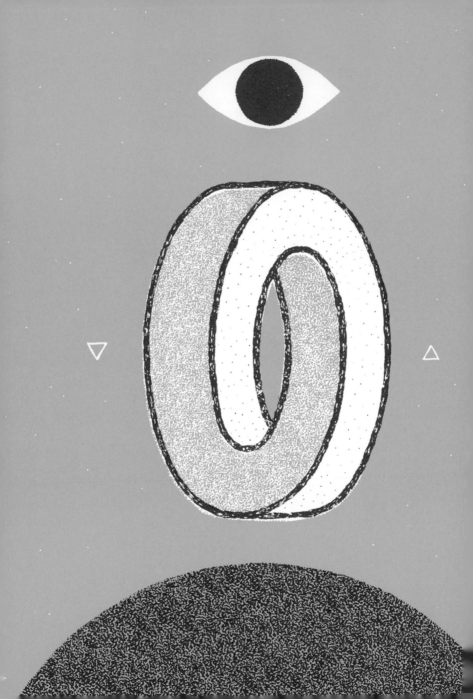

VI. Compatibility

Is life with a partner, friend, colleague or neighbour going to be harmonious? Or will it be more like grinding gears? This chapter simplifies astrological compatibility, focusing simply on signs. But as you've found out in previous chapters, there's more to astrology than that.

To really test your compatibility with someone, you need to scratch beneath the surface – start by creating a birth chart for yourself, and then the person you want to match with. As usual, identify where the planets are positioned (in which signs and houses), but focus particularly on the personal planets (Sun, Moon, Venus, Mercury and Mars).

Compare Moon signs to reveal emotional compatibility, Mercury for communication, Venus for love and Mars for desire and action. The sign the planet is in will inform how to read that planet. For example, your Venus (love) in Aries (assertive) will mean you're forthright in love. If your partner has Mars (action) in Gemini (communicative), you might find your assertive adoration matches their flirty style.

Finally, note the element of each sign, as this also comes into play. And go even further by looking at the Mode, too.

No signs apart/ same sign (conjunct)
Kindred spirits

ARIES Aries
TAURUS Taurus
GEMINI Gemini
CANCER Cancer
LEO Leo
VIRGO Virgo

LIBRA Libra
SCORPIO Scorpio
SAGITTARIUS Sagittarius
CAPRICORN Capricorn
AQUARIUS Aquarius
PISCES Pisces

Birds of a feather flock together in this mutual appreciation club. You both share so much in common it's easy to get along. Because you share a sign (element and mode) you will feel familiar to each other and share a similar energy. The more planets you share in the same signs, the more familiar you will feel to each other. Sometimes it's refreshing to come home to that kind of natural understanding, acceptance and validation. The down side, if there is one, is that you won't extend yourself or be forced to learn through difference.

Example match

Virgo with Virgo
You both love order and cleanliness, this is a no-brainer for living together. Your work styles are in harmony as well. You both need quiet time out, as well as routine and a healthy lifestyle. Problems only emerge if you have different ways of achieving the same results, so find the same road and walk it together.

Both have the Sun in the same sign

This makes relating to each other easy as you share similar traits. Most of all, you share the same sort of vitality and energy, similar interests light you up and you shine in a similar way.

Different planets in the same sign

Moon with Venus

This is a beautiful combo. the planet of emotions cuddled up with the planet of love in the same sign. This literally feels good – it feels like love and probably is. This combo is the cherry on top that will soften most disagreements and give you a very loving place to lean into when more difficult aspects are triggered.

One sign apart (semi-sextile)
Look a little closer

ARIES Pisces, Taurus
TAURUS Aries, Gemini
GEMINI Taurus, Cancer
CANCER Gemini, Leo
LEO Cancer, Virgo
VIRGO Leo, Libra

LIBRA Virgo, Scorpio
SCORPIO Libra, Sagittarius
SAGITTARIUS Scorpio, Capricorn
CAPRICORN Sagittarius, Aquarius
AQUARIUS Capricorn, Pisces
PISCES Aquarius, Aries

You'll have to dig to find the hidden commonalities, however they do exist. You both have psychologically different ways of understanding and operating in the world. You can learn a lot from each other and contribute to some impressive personal growth. A fascinating combo if you're both willing to step back and appreciate each other's differences rather than mould one another into your image or style. Once you manage to 'see' each other, you can have each other's blind spots covered and open up ways of seeing the world from an entirely new perspective. Do that, and you'll make a formidable team. For more detail, check the element of each person to reveal the best way to approach them.

Example match

Sagittarius with Scorpio

Watery Scorpio has the depth, BS detector and ability to create intimacy. She can teach Fire sign Sagittarius about deeper feelings and how to face them, as well as accept and transform loss. She opens up a whole new level of esoteric and hidden truth that can be fascinating to the knowledge seeker.

Sagittarius brings inspiration, light and expansion to Scorpio who can become entrenched in her cavernous underworld emotions or stuck in labyrinthine thoughts. The Fire and movement of Sagittarius lifts her up, encouraging her to bring her knowledge into the open.

Two signs apart (sextile)
Just add water

ARIES Aquarius, Gemini
TAURUS Pisces, Cancer
GEMINI Aries, Leo
CANCER Taurus, Virgo
LEO Gemini, Libra
VIRGO Cancer, Scorpio

LIBRA Leo, Sagittarius
SCORPIO Virgo, Capricorn
SAGITTARIUS Libra, Aquarius
CAPRICORN Scorpio, Pisces
AQUARIUS Sagittarius, Aries
PISCES Capricorn, Taurus

This combo takes the slightest push to activate some beautiful synergy that can be palpable. The Fire and Air signs combine, while the Earth and Water signs join hands so everyone's paired with their best psychological matches. Compatible elements that easily stimulate and feed one another. Most enjoyable!

Example matches

Leo with Libra
Libra loves to adore and Leo loves to be adored. Leo loves to romance and Libra values relationships, beauty and love highly. A charming, light, effervescent and glamorous pairing.

Pisces with Capricorn or Taurus
Both Capricorn and Taurus are Earth signs, therefore they bring stability and containment to Watery, emotional and creative Pisces. Pisces softens both the Earth signs in a way that helps them connect emotionally, relax, become more fluid and express their own creativity. She gives them someone to provide for and a reason for their worldly endeavours.

Three signs apart (square)
Dynamic duo or grinding gears

ARIES Capricorn, Cancer
TAURUS Aquarius, Leo
GEMINI Pisces, Virgo
CANCER Aries, Libra
LEO Taurus, Scorpio
VIRGO Gemini, Sagittarius

LIBRA Cancer, Capricorn
SCORPIO Leo, Aquarius
SAGITTARIUS Virgo, Pisces
CAPRICORN Libra, Aries
AQUARIUS Scorpio, Taurus
PISCES Sagittarius, Gemini

This is the most challenging yet charged pairing. The tension and energy of the square will fascinate and magnetise you to each other. However, conscious effort is required to direct all that energy so it doesn't combust in a clash of the titans. Accept and appreciate each other's differences. Look at what you can learn from the element and sign – can this help you find common ground?

It might be time to check your planets: if you have a lot of planets three signs apart (square), you'll be in for a constant battle. Enter at your own risk and be willing to do the work – or bow out gracefully. If you manage this combo, you'll be like two stallions pulling a chariot – you'll be highly charged and accomplish more than you could alone.

Example match

Scorpio with Aquarius
Scorpio is deep and highly tuned to all the unspoken emotion in herself and others. She requires total loyalty, needs to merge and absolutely needs you to have her back emotionally. Aquarius wants space, detachment and needs to communicate feelings in order to understand them. These two signs are so different, yet Scorpio can help Aquarius get in touch with her emotions. Aquarius can assist Scorpio to become more objective. You'll need to be highly aware, committed and willing to communicate in order to make this work.

Four signs apart (trine)
Easy street

FIRE Aries, Leo, Sagittarius   **AIR** Gemini, Libra, Aquarius
EARTH Taurus, Virgo, Capricorn   **WATER** Cancer, Scorpio, Pisces

You are both the same element, so naturally feel a familiar vibe in each other's company. Psychologically you operate on a similar wavelength. This combo is harmonious and so easy. Cruise and enjoy. Check your planets: if they are four signs apart, it can be straightforward and easygoing. But if there are too many planets that are positioned four signs apart, you'll lack the tension to propel you forward or make change, and things can become rather lazy and indulgent.

Example matches

Pisces with Cancer
You are both Water signs so you can indulge in feelings without having to explain yourselves. Your connection is virtually psychic and you feel understood and cared for. Both are sensitive signs: this is a sweet and loving combo.

Pisces with Scorpio
This is a match made in heaven. You swim together in emotional bliss, shutting out the rest of the world. Almost too much of a good thing. You are both long-term lovers and you'll never forget each other no matter the course your lives take. This can be an escapist or highly creative match.

Five signs apart (quincunx/inconjunct)
Find common ground

ARIES Scorpio, Virgo
TAURUS Sagittarius, Libra
GEMINI Capricorn, Scorpio
CANCER Aquarius, Sagittarius
LEO Pisces, Capricorn
VIRGO Aries, Aquarius

LIBRA Taurus, Pisces
SCORPIO Aries, Gemini
SAGITTARIUS Taurus, Cancer
CAPRICORN Gemini, Leo
AQUARIUS Cancer, Virgo
PISCES Leo, Libra

While each of these signs have an affinity with each other, it's rather hidden and difficult to find. Keep looking and you'll discover treasure. You're so different, yet you can make it work once you identify what you have in common. Appreciate your differences, make adjustments, yet don't try to change the other or yourself to fit. There can be friction if you do.

Example match

Taurus with Sagittarius
A hidden affinity you both share is a love of nature. Make sure you embrace this aspect and try camping, walking or spending time in the great outdoors together. Travel together and make sure you include lots of food, outdoors, pampering and exotica. Taurus makes sure plans are viable, while Sagittarius provides the inspiration and go power needed to get those plans off the ground. These combos offer so much more than either initially thought was possible. Stay mindful of differences so you can broaden your collective arsenal of talent.

Six signs apart (opposition)
Bicycle built for two, requires balance

ARIES Libra
TAURUS Scorpio
GEMINI Sagittarius
CANCER Capricorn
LEO Aquarius
VIRGO Pisces

LIBRA Aries
SCORPIO Taurus
SAGITTARIUS Gemini
CAPRICORN Cancer
AQUARIUS Leo
PISCES Virgo

Opposites really do attract. You both represent extreme ends in polarity of the same spectrum which means you'll be looking in the mirror at qualities that would be beneficial for you to develop in yourself. This is an opportunity to round yourself out – if you don't, you'll rely on each other to each be a wheel on the bicycle for it to work. Which is also fun!

You feed each other in a way that can be understood and appreciated. Balance is a key to this pairing so make sure you give a little time to each person's needs. When harmony is struck, this can be an enduring combo.

Example match

Leo with Aquarius
Find balance: Leo, it can't always be all about you and your emotions raging and roaring; Aquarius, not everything needs to be lived through high concept alone. Leo can learn some detachment from Air sign Aquarius. Leo is comfortable with her instincts teaching Aquarius how to let go of the larger group dynamic and go with her own flow.

VII. Transits

You've fired up your inner mystic with the ancient knowledge of astrology and you've learnt to read your birth chart – so what's next? Well, the future of course!

You might want a bit more insight into when and what is happening in your life and how you're responding to it. You might want to know when love could be calling. Or understand why your work seems to be going really well, and therefore how and when to maximise your efforts to make the most of that cosmic flow. You don't need to employ blind hope… it's all foretold in the cyclic revolution of the planets as they move through the sky and interact with your birth chart – this movement is otherwise known as the planet's transits.

Transits are like cosmic signposts that will help you read a situation or coming event, and give you an idea of how you will handle it. To determine a transit, you need your birth chart, and then you need to know where the planets are on a given day – that could be today, or it could be a future day. It could be a day that correlates to some astro buzz terms, such as Mercury retrograde, Saturn return, New Moon and Full Moon.

You can create a current or future chart in the same way as you would a birth chart – use the online tool at www.astroallstarz.com/birthchart. When you overlay these two charts, you'll see the transiting planets forming aspects (see page 165) with a planet or house in your birth chart.

Transiting planets in aspect with a planet in your birth chart

I'm using the planet Uranus (revolution, change and originality) to demonstrate how a planet in transit can signify change when forming an aspect to a point in your birth chart.

Transiting Uranus conjunct Venus in your birth chart
The element of surprise and sudden change that Uranus brings to your natal planet of love will affect your love life and relationships – you can expect high voltage! Conjunct means 'merged functions', so you could meet someone with Uranian qualities or just fall madly in love complete with electricity and sparks. You will be on fire and feel like a real live wire. A very exciting time!

Transiting Uranus square Venus in your birth chart
Squares are dynamic and challenging – often signifying an area or time you're being pushed to grow in. There might be a relationship in your life you are feeling challenged by, but are resisting changing. The more you resist Uranus (change) the more psychologically painful it will be. Let go or dramatically change the way you are dealing with the relationship.

Uranus transiting the 4th House in your birth chart
The 4th House represents home and private self, so expect change and renewel (Uranus) on the home front. You'll likely move residence at this time or you may give your home a radical makeover. Perhaps new ways of living will appeal, especially if it's communal or co-operative.

Uranus transiting the 10th House in your birth chart
The 10th House represents career and reputation. With the revolutionary vibes of Uranus in transit, you'll be a step ahead in your career and looking into how to use the latest tech and social networking to improve your public image. You may completely change careers at this time. Your image will undergo a radical shift. Go with it!

Planets in retrograde

Retrograde refers to a time when a planet appears to be moving backwards (as opposed to direct motion), due to the relative orbiting speeds of Earth versus the other planets. All planets have retrograde periods except the Sun and Moon. Think of retrogrades as an interval; time to take a break and see what the cosmic tide washes up before resuming the show. For example:

Mercury retrograde

Arguably the most well-known astrology term, Mercury retrograde is all about reviewing anything and everything to do with communications. This includes anything written or verbalised, devices that relay information, people or even things such as mobile phones, transport and travel.

Mercury retrogrades 3–4 times a year for approximately 3.5 weeks. During this time, you need to review, rethink and retool rather than take action on decisions, book trips, buy a new phone or sign a contract. If you must, then triple check everything! The crux of Merc retro is that new information comes to light during this period that can see you recalibrating plans or redoing work.

The area of your birth chart Mercury is in during its retrograde gives you more information about where to expect some revision or pandemonium. If it aspects any planets in your chart, especially the inner/personal planets, then that particular transit will be more likely to show up as events in your life.

Mercury retrograde in the 7th House of your birth chart

The 7th house is all about one-on-one equal partnerships such as marriage, business partners and contracts. Therefore, don't plan a wedding or sign a contract until the retrograde period is over. More info about your intended may come to light during this period, the wedding may be cancelled or interrupted!

Planetary returns

A return refers to a planet that has completed an entire cycle through the zodiac and has returned to the exact point in your birth chart that it was in at the moment you were born. All planets with an orbit that falls within our lifetime will have a return. For example, our birthday sees the Sun complete a full cycle around the zodiac, returning, for one day only, to the exact degree of the sign it was in the day we were born. And Mars has a two-year orbit, so we have a Mars return every two years. Returns indicate a completion of one cycle of what that planet represents, and the beginning of the next stage of growth in that area. The planet indicates what will be felt, the sign is how it will be felt, and the house is the area of life where you will feel it.

Moon phases

Use the Moon's phases – from New Moon (when all is dark) to Full Moon (when it is bright in the sky) – in partnership with intentions and manifestations. On the New Moon, plant the seeds of your intentions, just as farmers have done for thousands of years. When there is little light, the seed sends its roots into the soil. As the light of the Moon grows, the seed then sends its leaves up to meet the light. Our intentions are set and take root in our subconscious, so we don't have to rely purely on the rational, conscious mind to make the change we desire. This is manifesting. As the Moon moves through its phases, our intentions manifest. Fine-tune your intentions by noting the sign that the New Moon is in, and its placement in your birth chart. Do this, and you'll be cooking on gas!

> ### New Moon in Capricorn in the 8th House of your birth chart
> Set intentions that relate to Capricorn (career). And then combine it with the 8th House (shared resources, sex and death). For example, your intention may be to create a business project with someone. Aim high for what you desire, don't let your 'sensible' inner critic dilute your intentions. As with all of astrology, approach it with an open mind and an open heart – let astrology be the scaffolding and your inner voice, your guiding light.

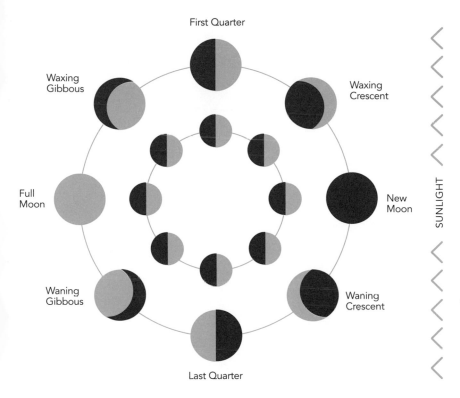

First Quarter

Waxing
Gibbous

Waxing
Crescent

Full
Moon

New
Moon

Waning
Gibbous

Waning
Crescent

Last Quarter

SUNLIGHT

Further reading / Partial bibliography

Astrological Source Book
by Jeannette Lewis-Hill,
Orion Acadamy press, 2004

The Confidence Code, The Science and Art of Self-Assurance – What Women Should Know
by Katty Kay and Claire Shipman,
Harper Collins, 2014

A Handbook of Medical Astrology
by Jane Ridder-Patrick, Crab Apple
Press, 2nd Edition, 2006

The Mind/Body Code, How to Change the Beliefs that Limit your Health, Longevity and Success,
by Dr Mario Martinez,
Sounds True, 2014

The Psychodynamics of Inconjunctions,
by Allen Epstein, Samuel Weiser Inc,
1984

The Knot of Time, Astrology and the Female Experience,
by Lindsay River and Sally Gillespie,
The Womens Press Ltd, 1987

Symbols for Women, a Feminist Guide to the Zodiac, by Sheila Farrant,
Mandala, 1989

www.astroallstarz.com – make your own free astrological birth chart, order reports on your birth chart or book a personal astrological consultation.
www.cafeastrology.com – an easy-to-understand, comprehensive site.

www.astro.com – an advanced and comprehensive site that includes more than you'll ever need to know.

There are a wealth of astrology writers that have paved the way for our contemporary style of astrology. Some of these are Liz Green, Robert Hand, Howard Sasportas, Tracey Marks, Jan Spiller, Steven Forrest. I recommend most contributions by these writers. The Theosophical Society has centres, bookshops and libraries in many cities and countries. They have a selection of astrology texts as well as other metaphysical and philosophical books to help you on your quest for expansion, truth and self knowledge. There is an official astrological governing body in most countries, which run large international conventions, as well as groups, workshops and seminars.

Contact your nearest body for more information:

Australia – *www.faainc.org.au*
America – *www.astrologers.com*
Britain – *www.professionalastrologers.co.uk*

Acknowledgements

To you dear reader, for your willingness to explore astrology, explore yourself and be open to connecting with your highest potential. Thank you to those seekers who embrace the duality in all things and are willing to do the work to integrate.

Thank you to my learned astrology teachers Glennys Lawton and Brian Clark at Astro*Synthesis and Stella Woods, aka Stella Starwoman. Isobel Lambert for initially introducing me to the wonders of astrology via Suzanne White's book *The New Astrology*. Amanda Mills for leading the way and encouraging me to study astrology formally.

Thank you to the rapidly growing collective of astrology enthusiasts and practitioners pulling astrology out of an archaic patriarchal lens, salvaging the best and transforming the rest, and for contributing to the development of astrology for the modern woman.

Thank you to all those who have loved, encouraged and inspired me along the way, as well as those who have called me out, forcing me to level up in my craft and find my determination.

Felicity Lawless for lighting the way and inspiring me by walking your talk, moving me into flow with your gift of love, an open heart and an open creative mind. Chelsea Rheese for continuing to research and explore the metaphysical world, sharing your teachings and contributing to my knowledge, while pushing me through resistance. Rebecca Hartley for being my go-to rock of support and design hero. My cousin Fiona for providing a calm, stable and loving family studio to work from. Claire Howell for sharing your chart and story as an example. Nicole Rose for being the can-do Cappy who always aims for solution to any challenge.

Lastly, a big thank you to Zena Alkayat for creating this precious opportunity to share this ancient system of knowledge. And for applying your modern feminist perspective in a tangible way and helping to redefine astrology from a modern, female-centric lens through your work in publishing. Thank you Giulia Garbin for updating astrology visually with your fabulous design skills, and thanks to the editorial and publicity teams who worked so hard. Thank you to everyone at Quadrille for bringing your best and making *Star Power* happen for modern mystics everywhere.

PUBLISHING DIRECTOR Sarah Lavelle
COMMISSIONING EDITOR Zena Alkayat
DESIGN AND ILLUSTRATION Giulia Garbin
DESIGN ASSISTANT Florian Michelet
PRODUCTION DIRECTOR Vincent Smith
PRODUCTION CONTROLLER Tom Moore

Published in 2018 by Quadrille,
an imprint of Hardie Grant Publishing

Quadrille
52 – 54 Southwark Street
London SE1 1UN
quadrille.com

Reprinted in 2018
10 9 8 7 6 5 4 3 2

ISBN 978 1 78713 224 5

Printed in China

Planets

⊙ Sun

☽ Moon

☿ Mercury

♀ Venus

♂ Mars

♃ Jupiter

♄ Saturn

⚷ Chiron

♅ Uranus

♆ Neptune

♇ Pluto

Signs

♈ Aries

♉ Taurus

♊ Gemini

♋ Cancer

♌ Leo

♍ Virgo

♎ Libra

♏ Scorpio

♐ Sagittarius

♑ Capricorn

♒ Aquarius

♓ Pisces

Elements

◊ Fire

▽ Earth

△ Air

◊ Water

Modes

⫲ Cardinal

⬡ Fixed

⚏ Mutable